THE ROUGH GUIDE TO

bb-27

Credits

Contributing Editor: Donald Hutera
Editor: (Rough Guides): Allen Robertson
Editorial Consultant (Rough Guides): Andrew Lockett
Contributors: Jenny Gilbert, Keith Watson, Lyndsey Winship,
Arts Council England, MJW Productions, www.londondance.com
Foreword by Michael Nunn and William Trevitt, George Piper Dances
Image Collation: Hans de Kretser
Production: John McKay
Layout: Katie Pringle
Cover Design: David Wearn
Proofreading: Diane Margolis
Commissioned by Arts Council England
Project Managed by Jacqueline Rose, Arts Council England
with Anne Beresford

Project managed on behalf of Rough Guides by Remote World Ltd

Publishing Information

First edition – June 2004
Published by Rough Guides Ltd
80 Strand, London WC2R 0RL
Email: mail@roughguides.co.uk

Printed in Italy by LegoPrint S.p.A.

The publishers and authors have done their best to ensure the accuracy
and currency of all the information in *The Rough Guide to Choreography*.

ISBN 1-84353-430-4

The Rough Guide to Choreography is a television series devised
and introduced by Michael Nunn and William Trevitt, directed by
Beadie Finzi and produced by MJW Productions for Channel 4.

Contents

Foreword

As a dancer there's nothing more rewarding than having a role choreographed for you. It will be crafted to perfectly fit your skills and gifts, your temperament and qualities. In the hands of a talented choreographer you will be challenged to explore the limits of your ability.

When we founded George Piper Dances in 1999, it was with a simple and selfish aim: to seek out new and interesting choreographers to make dances for us. We had already been privileged to work with several of the great choreographers of the twentieth century – Frederick Ashton, Kenneth MacMillan, William Forsythe, to name a few. But, greedily, we wanted more. Now in a position to actually commission work in which we would dance, we became aware of the satisfaction of a true collaboration. We were awakened to the thrill of exploration and creative freedom that we found in improvisation, of finding inspiration in the most unexpected places.

We have thrived on sharing ideas and knowledge with some of the most gifted choreographers working today, often in a cross-pollination of styles. These experiences have filled us with an evangelical desire to share the normally unseen, private time spent in the studio between choreographer and dancer with an audience. Most fascinating for us is their varied techniques. It may be the manipulation of everyday movement, or borrowing ideas from martial arts. It might be improvisation, or the absorption of street and club moves. All are valid, and each practitioner has his or her own way of working. The key is inspiration, no matter where it comes from.

Of course we've only just begun. There are a great many wonderful choreographers working in dance, film and theatre that we would still dearly love to work with, but at least we've made a start. So far we can only offer you a glimpse into the work of a few of these artists, but it's a glimpse from close-up and one that's brimming with respect for a very ephemeral art.

love
Michael & Billy

Michael Nunn and William Trevitt of George Piper Dances

Introduction

"There should be no art form more accessible than dance, yet no art is more mystifying in the public imagination." The words belong to Twyla Tharp. This driven American choreographer has spent forty-odd years successfully smudging the line that divides high and popular art. Whether her work is praised or reviled, there's no doubt that Tharp knows her stuff. "Dance," she has written, "is simply the refinement of human movement – walking, running and jumping. We are all experts."

It's a neat formula: I move, therefore I dance. But what you *do* with your, or others', moves is another matter altogether. That's what the art of choreography is all about. What we've tried to do in this small volume is uncover some of the motivations and methods behind that art. It's the same territory that George Piper Dances' Michael Nunn and William Trevitt, aka 'The Ballet Boyz', set out to explore in their Channel 4 series *The Rough Guide to Choreography*. For them the challenge was to learn all they could about the bewilderingly varied approaches to making a dance, and then to put their asses on the line by actually creating one themselves. What's more, their dance is intended for the widest possible public consumption via television.

Whether this was a brave or foolhardy act, only time – and audiences and critics – will tell. The fact remains: Michael's and Billy's quest was a major kick-start for this little book. Treat it as a compact and by no means comprehensive taster of a big subject. Ideally, it will serve as a user-friendly cousin of the series, providing entertaining insights into how, why and where choreography has been done, and by whom. Dip into it and pick up a smattering of information about what influences confound and inspire dance-makers past and present.

Donald Hutera, Editor

What's This?

Choreography inside and out

People ask, "How do you make a dance?" My answer is simple. "Put yourself in motion."

Twyla Tharp in her autobiography *Push Comes to Shove*

Dancing is a vital and innately human activity. Our urge to move, it would seem, is genetically encoded. It's why we kick in the womb. Dance is also irreducibly individual. Ashley Killar, London-born former artistic director of Royal New Zealand Ballet, conducted workshops with children in Bantu settlements in equatorial Africa. He learned that there is a Bantu greeting in which people say not "How do you do?" but "How do you dance?"

The universe itself is dancing and some people make it their business to select from this virtually endless source of raw material and harness its rhythms into some kind of order. We call this choreography.

Out of Thin Air

"Pedantically, choreography is the art of making dances," says *Guardian* dance critic Judith Mackrell. "Putting steps together. Making patterns out of the steps. But obviously the way that people approach choreography, the way they think about it and define it, changes radically from artist to artist."

And choreographers, she continues, "are people who, from their own bodies, from thin air... invent puzzles for themselves that they're going to solve through putting movement together. They have a story to tell, or patterns they want to compose onstage, or pieces of music that they want to turn into dance.

"They tend not to be household names," she continues, "the way that a few stellar ballerinas and male dancers are. But evidently without a choreographer you have no dance. The choreographer is like the composer, and the dancers are the musicians. You can't just have a bunch of musicians in an orchestra pit playing whatever comes into their heads. The choreographers give the dancers the steps to dance. He or she invents the story or canvas which the dancers populate."

Instinct and Talent

In order to fulfil this function, Mackrell believes, "You have to be born with some kind of instinct that makes you want to translate the world into movement. You also have to be someone who knows the fundamentals of the body. You may not be a very good dancer yourself, but you have to have the equipment of dance language that you've learnt and a sense of what the body can do."

Ballet genius George Balanchine advised budding dance-makers to join a dance company, the traditional meeting ground for conductors, musicians, designers and other dancers. "The object of the dancer's technical training is to enable him to perform, with perfect ease, choreographic movements... not limited by considerations of practical, daily life. He uses his technical proficiency to express in movement his essential knowledge." But, he cautioned, you can't teach talent. "There is no school that can teach choreography, just as there is no school where you can learn to be a novelist or a poet."

Organised Mayhem

Traditionally, choreography happens when a group of people learn and absorb one person's work so many hours per day. As Mackrell pointed out, there are as many motives for this collective activity as there are people. Dances can reflect the speed and complexity of technology-led modern life, or just as easily hark back to primitive impulses. Some dances are sparked off by literature or myth, others by the visual arts. Some expose the emotional and psychological working of human character, while others draw upon animal behaviour.

While artists tend to know what they hope to achieve, sometimes they don't know quite how they're going to go about it. No wonder choreographer Christopher Wheeldon refers to what he does as "organised mayhem". There are so many other choices to be made about music, whether newly-commissioned or pre-recorded, plus sets, costumes, lighting. And what to call the piece? Titles are important, although often that won't be decided until near the end of the creation period.

From Lips and Limbs

Above all else, who will you get to do your dance? Many choreographers hold auditions. Others see a lot of dance, and invite the performers who most interest or intrigue them onstage to become their interpreters or collaborators. Twyla Tharp says she knows if a dancer is right for her from the moment they walk through the door and cross the room to meet her. It's like love at first sight.

Some choreographers have used miniature figures or objects to plot out movement in advance. Others draw it all out of their own bodies, or those of their dancers. One of Lea Anderson's dancers has said that all of Anderson's

Beadie Finzi filming William Trevitt from George Piper Dances for the Channel 4 series *The Rough Guide to Choreography*

choreography issued directly "from her lips and limbs". She keeps a notebook of thoughts and images that relate directly to each dance she's making and uses this to suggest and trigger movement. Similarly, Siobhan Davies treats her dancers as co-creators, setting up situations that are conducive to discovering ways of moving neither she nor they had thought of before.

Cultural Climates

Dance tends to come out of an artist's personality and environment – a mixture of intelligence and instinct, as dance is a distillation of everything a choreographer is or has experienced. For instance, a rhythm on the streets in Brazil – in the interactions between people, in their bodies and their response to climate, music and all the other myriad cultural influences – is palpable onstage in, say, the work of dance-maker Deborah Colker, from Rio de Janeiro. Another prime example is Finland, where the dances have qualities of subtlety and wit, stillness, and a sensitivity to the use of stage lighting unique to that country. It's possible to gain almost as much insight into what shapes Finnish dance-making by having a traditional sauna as it is by seeing a performance.

Cooks and Atoms

To sum up, the motivational fuel for dance-making is burning desire, natural talent and a great deal of curiosity. A willingness to experiment, regardless of mistakes that may get made, is likewise valuable. The training and study never stop. Whatever triggers new perspectives or fresh thought, or poses a challenge, is what counts. "You must be able to be inventive at any time," Balanchine wrote. "You can't be like the cook who can cook only two dishes: you must be able to cook them all."

Most choreographers would like hungry audiences to savour their work. A major stumbling block is the perception of the art form as difficult or impenetrable. "People think that dance is a language that nobody can get," Mackrell says. "There's a huge amount of brainwork that goes on, but it's also a very physical, hands-on process."

It is perhaps best to first absorb a dance experience. Specialist knowledge is not required. Do you worry about your inability to play this, that or the other instrument when listening to music, or your lack of cinematography skills when you go to a film? Dance is no different.

"In a good piece of dance I expect there to be stuff that keeps me awake, keeps me looking, keeps me listening," Mackrell says. The impact can be enormous. "You know if the world changes on its axis and you come out feeling like your atoms have been rearranged."

Here is a cross-section of comments, most by choreographers about themselves and their various takes on aspects of their common – or, better, uncommon – profession.

It's like coffee. It never tastes as good as it smells.
– George Balanchine after a premiere

A kind of writing in dance.
– Jonathan Burrows, asked "What is choreography?"

Why do we care so dreadfully? In order to communicate. With whomever will listen. To say what lies behind language.
– Agnes de Mille

Agnes had a broad range of references on which to draw. Her firsthand experience encompassed city and country, East and West, theatre and film. She had studied the arts, especially painting and sculpture. She was knowledgeable about world history, particularly with regard to customs, costumes, manners and morals. Her specific gift was her ability to find the precise gesture that conveyed a universal emotion and express it through a specific character in a specific time, rhythm and place.
– from Carol Eastman's Agnes de Mille biography, *No Intermissions*, 1996

I was 13. My parents had just divorced. I'd wanted to take dance classes prior to that, but my father was definitely not interested in that idea. My mother told me just the other day that her alimony payments were what paid for my initial classes. Within six months I had a scholarship. Eventually I went to Juilliard and then came to Dance Theatre of Harlem where I danced for fourteen seasons. I stopped because I wanted to choreograph, but it was about time anyway. I was 36, and I've no regrets. I was never one for performing, actually. I preferred the process, you know, working in the studio, which a lot of people hate. I love it. It's so special – making things grow, bringing something to life. I sometimes call myself a dance architect. I'm building houses for dancers to live in, structures for the dancers where they can go inside – they know where the sofa is, they know where the phone is – and get comfortable.

– Robert Garland, choreographer and former dancer of Dance Theatre of Harlem

Good text. Space. Rhythm. Bodies. Music. It's enough. You don't need anything else.

– Maguy Marin's recipe for artistic success

Dance and boxing aren't as opposite as people think. Both are physical articulations. A phrase [in dance] is like a combination and a boxer, like a dancer, only has his/her body. In the lights and in the ring/stage there is nowhere to hide, every mistake is obvious... and both dancers and boxers are underpaid.

– Sports and dance publicist Tony Shepherd

When I started making work, instead of idealising the body I wanted to explore it, to show it in another way than we'd seen in the 1980s: athletic, virtuosic, superhuman. I was working with vulnerability, frailty, doubt and distortion.

– American expatriate Meg Stuart

I'm a little leery of the word 'inspiration'. I like the word 'deadline' better.

– American choreographer Paul Taylor

LEA ANDERSON

What is choreography?

Whatever you intend it to mean. It seems funny to have an opinion about it when it doesn't really matter, because it's really about what other people think it is... I dislike people who call themselves directors because it seems that you're not giving any credit to the movement, and the movement is what I'm interested in. I've heard enough people talking and shouting onstage, it's quite tedious. But I haven't seen enough people moving onstage yet. So I don't know what to call myself. Dance-maker? I wish I had a proper name, like a plumber. No dispute what they do.

On the pitfalls of training

How come you can be taught how to make visual art, and music, and writing? But dance ... They don't teach you to look! They're confused as to what the most important thing is, good technical dancing or a coherent visual idea developed in front of you in movement.

LAURIE BOOTH

On life-time learning

After an improvisation I once said to Steve Paxton, "Wow, that was great!" and he said, "It's only taken thirty years to make that piece."

On the site of fresh sight

If you think about it, the human body is so limited. In every culture, in every moment in history, in every place, it's still the same shape. It's the object which is most deeply familiar, so as a choreographer the challenge is always, how do you get people to look at it as if they've never seen it before?

MATTHEW BOURNE

On dance without words

Apart from the musicals that I've worked on, I've never used speech in the dance pieces I've done because it always felt like I've failed if I've had to fall back on saying something with words rather than movement.

On making work

I'm always trying to improve and make the movement richer. I always know the music I'm using inside out. I surround myself with people who'll make something work, and not need to be told what to do all the time. It's about feeding them as much information as possible about who they are and the background of what we're doing.

ROSEMARY BUTCHER

On vision

It has never interested me that dance should be expressive in an emotional way. Movement in itself, placed against either an environment or other people, is my real interest, and in a way that is natural and free from too much affectation.

For me it's less about dance movement and more about the way in which ideas connected to the body can be performed and set up and looked at, but always based in the premise of someone's philosophy behind it. It's extremely easy to sling some steps together. But it's about the vision and intention behind it. And that's the thing you can't learn.

Which expression?

I think I see work visually as a whole, as a landscape. I choreograph because that's the craft I have, but actually it could be expressed through paint or sculpture. If I had the skills, then those mediums would suit me better.

What does a choreographer do?

Works with a physicality to make a visual performance. Creates art and art work using a dancing body. You start with a thing that's very important to you, an idea or a memory or an ongoing obsession which has the momentum to be explored. Memory's always extremely important. Your own place, your own culture, your own background. Your own desires, your own fears. Things that are incredibly close to your own self. You've got to use what you know. But it's re-examining what you know. That's how you open other doors to new investigations.

MERCE CUNNINGHAM

On unpredictability

One reason the dances are particularly difficult to see is that they are not constructed linearly. One thing doesn't lead to another. As a student in dance composition, I was taught that you led up to something, some climax. That didn't interest me very much. I rather liked the idea of things staying separate, something not leading up to something else. The continuity is constantly unpredictable rather than as though you were being led up a path.

On what interests him

How to place yourself in an unknown situation, and then find a solution, a way out of it. For me the subject of dance is dancing itself. It is not meant to represent something else, whether psychological, literary, or aesthetic. It relates much more to everyday experience, daily life, watching people as they move in the streets.

– from *The Dancer and the Dance*, interviews with Jacqueline Lesschaeve, 1985.

SIOBHAN DAVIES

On information

Even if they can't say 'I really understood that,' people like to watch. I don't know that they necessarily always get the choreography, but I think they like to watch dancers and they get information from that. Because there's a language about how people move which, if they're genuinely accurate about what they're doing, starts to give information.

On breaking habits

We have habit in our bodies. You feel comfortable with the moves you do. It's how to remove yourself slightly from that knowledge, and find out that you probably look very good doing some other move that your body doesn't feel comfortable in, but it's real and accurate to the situation.

Find out where movement sits differently in the body. All thinking happens on two legs. All movements, if you are not careful, start with your two legs down. How do you start working from other places than that? What conversations can you have with different parts of the body? Can you put two rhythms together? If you have a pattern in the arms, what happens if you have that same pattern in your hips? It doesn't have to make a movement, but you start discovering what your tools are.

On the job of the choreographer

I am the editor, the director. I support the dancers as I can, and choose what I think is true to the task rather than general movement. My job is to coach it out and to throw away. We throw away masses. Our tendency as artists is to do too much: "When in doubt do a bit more." Whereas, in truth, when in doubt probably do a bit less. Take something away. Show what you want to show. But be clear about what you mean to do.

You need to find a structure, a form, an emotion that would interest you. If I find the emotion too early on, I am trying to service that emotion. And then you make movement for that emotion. Whereas my purpose is to try and make the piece and find what it is as it's getting closer. The subject just simply arrives. I find it by making the work.

On the audience

I do think of them as a particular, not a general, audience. Each

Hubert Essakow, Oxana Panchenko, Monica Zamora. George Piper Dances

one has a very particular take on the work. If you try and think of them as individuals, then you are going to do particular work. If you start to think of them as a mass, then I think you start to make sort of mass work. The clearer you are the more likely they are to appreciate it. The truth is nobody feels what you felt. They are not going to feel that weight rushing around in your body. But they will get something else. So one of your jobs is to try and make as clear as possible the feeling.

What can dance do?

Don't try and do anything dance can't do. Dance very easily can fall into the big subjects – love, death, war. But it doesn't do that, I personally think, very well. Dance is sort of gorgeous in its particular way. It does all the subtle things, all those rather odd subjects, much better. It does spatial complexity incredibly well. Whereas the big stuff, Shakespeare does that. Or film.

PANAYOTIS SINNOS

– part of the Channel 4 series *The Rough Guide to Choreography*

BILL T. JONES

On identity

What kind of choreographer do I consider myself? It's a mischievous question most of us would rather not deal with. Most of us would say it's irrelevant. I guess I'm experimental because I try to put together disparate elements to see what happens, but I prefer to be called contemporary, which is a very humble way of saying that it's a work made now.

On choreographic challenge

What is the greatest challenge of choreographing? To overcome personal clichés as well as general clichés. What am I trying to get across to an audience? I would like to become more and more a force that is a voice of social consciousness, something that brings people together, or at least brings people to questioning – to make works that deeply affect people and yet are cool and distant enough so that they can be observed like a sculpture, as a presence is observed.

– from *Further Steps: Fifteen Choreographers on Modern Dance* by Connie Kreemer, 1987.

AKRAM KHAN

On his intentions

I don't have any ideas to communicate. I explore an idea conceptually in the initial stages and then go into a studio and let that idea go, not hold onto it but just trust subconsciously that it will be there and just see where I go with it. Not like a lot of choreographers who have an idea that they want the audience to clearly understand. For me that's not the fundamental point of the work. I feel it is a world for the audience to enter and to leave whenever they feel like.

On choreography

To know choreography is nothing at all. To imagine is everything. The word choreography carries a multitude of responsibilities. It is the creator, the dictator. It is the guide, the listener. And it is also the mother. To me, to choreograph is to be a storyteller.

RUSSELL MALIPHANT

What is choreography?

Using physical language to express an idea or take people's consciousness or imagination on a journey.

On reading the body

The body can be very clear, and quite often people can read it very well. Say you see someone walking down the street. You can see if they are a bit down, or jumping for joy. You can see it in the rhythm in which they're walking, or how their breath is moving through their body.

WAYNE MCGREGOR

On surfing

Audiences are very important, but it's impossible to make your work directly for them. It's my responsibility as a choreographer to communicate something, but I am very happy with a range of possible interpretations. I hope the audience 'surfs' the piece for images that connect with them on an emotional or physical level.

On his style

It is hybrid, isn't it? But it's got a very bizarre logic. I like hard, graphic lines that I manipulate into something else. I'm interested in how you draw something and then break or distort it. The eye doesn't have an easy ride. It's like a rollercoaster. Either the speed is disorientating, or the physical grammar. You see a line for a second, something you feel is concrete that you can almost grab hold of, and then all of a sudden it flies into something else. That boneless kind of choreography fascinates me.

On ballet – or not

There's a discipline in my work that's very related to the language of classical dance. But I don't have any ballet background at all. I really thought I detested it. Why, I have no idea. I hadn't seen that much, but I had a resistance to it. I've hardly done a ballet class in my life.

On making dance

So many people think choreography is just making up steps or movement, but it's more than that. I always have the concepts of my pieces and always select who I want to work with, whether it's the composer, animator, designers or dancers. How is it that all these elements interact, and what meanings will emerge? I think that kind of randomness – the accidents that emerge out of selective choices – is our experience of everyday life.

MARK MORRIS

On making work

I only choreograph to music. I study the score. I make up all of the actions in the studio with the dancers present. I don't know of any secret magic trick to make it happen otherwise.

Is the ability to choreograph an innate gift? Who knows? I knew at a very early age that I wanted to make up dances, so I did and I do.

GLEN TETLEY

What is choreography?

Someone asked Antony Tudor, 'What is choreography?' He said, 'Choreography is simply the individual quality of movement of the choreographer.' That's the best definition, because that's how you know that this person has an individual voice.

Dancer into choreographer

I think the best choreography is that which is instinctual and spontaneous, which you can't pre-create. It's one of the interesting and difficult things about choreography. You don't go into a solitary place by yourself. You're in front of other people. And hopefully you're going to open this place in yourself where the creativity will come out in a spontaneous way.

The first step is the most difficult. Then it becomes a dialogue. The movement you give the dancer is taken to a place that sparks something inside you: 'It's slightly changed, but that's good. I didn't think of that.' I like that creative relationship. I don't like working with somebody who says, 'Show me what to do.' I never liked being just a repetitive dancer doing standard vocabulary. I wanted to be the best dancer in the world and I wanted every choreographer to want to work with me. In a way that led to me becoming a choreographer. I guess you have to find a way to be two people at the same time, to say to yourself, 'Well, when you were dancing you knew the sort of things you wanted to dance.' As the choreographer you can create them.

TWYLA THARP

On the mystery of creation

When I go into a studio I know exactly what I want, but never quite how I'll get it. Each dance is a mystery story.

On the dancer as muse

One of the inspirations in my work is the trust my dancers show in consigning their bodies to me. To me as a choreographer, Sara [long-time collaborator Sara Rudner] offered the perfect instrument, a deeply intelligent dancer. Superbly trained, willing to try anything, to move with me into the 'white zone,' the open, scary void you occupy as you create a new piece.

CHRISTOPHER WHEELDON

On getting started

I know that I am only as good as each ballet I choreograph. When I go into the room at the beginning of creating a new work, I still feel just as nervous as I did the time before. New people, new challenges I've set myself – nervous excitement.

On dancers

The only way I like to work now is in collaboration with the dancers. You have to capture something of their spirit, their personalities, a little part of their soul. I think the only way you can truly create something poetic is by finding dancers who will inspire you.

Oxana Panchenko and William Trevitt in Christopher Wheeldon's
Mesmerics

Everybody Dance

From MTV to the pitch

Dance is all around us: on the street, in clubs, in TV ads, on video, on the football pitch. So why is it, if you put it in a theatre, the defences go up and people start worrying that they're not going to "get" it?

Somehow there's a feeling that – because all of us are dancers in our own way – there must be some mythical secret lying behind a dance show, some mystical technique that places it beyond our comprehension. Nothing could be further from the truth; though dance does itself no favours when it wraps itself in navel-gazing enigma.

When it comes down to it, dance is the most accessible art form there is. It's the one that all of us – who'll never write a song, start that novel or star in a Hollywood blockbuster – will attempt at some point, even if it's only at a big fat Greek wedding. Just take a look around you: everyone's doing it.

Praise Be to MTV

From Elvis's twitchy pelvis, Michael Jackson's moonwalk and Madonna's Vogue, all the way up to J-Lo's butt-shaking and Justin Timberlake's update on body-popping – put pop and dance together and you get some of the seminal images of popular culture. So why does dance get treated like the poor relation?

Anyone who has seen the work of genius that is the video for Fatboy Slim's *Praise You* will need little persuading that the pop promo is at the very forefront of choreographic invention. Modern dance doesn't get any funnier than this. Created by the hitherto unheralded Torrance Community Dance group, this is a dance spin on reality TV. Featuring a bunch of amateur performers going through their routine in a crowded cinema foyer, much to the bemusement/amusement of the passing punters, it's ingenuous to the point of heartbreak. The joy of movement, of just doing it, is communicated with cheery honesty.

Featured on heavy rotation on MTV, *Praise You* has been instrumental in bringing the dance virtues of the pop video some long-overdue recognition. No longer dismissed as

ALISTAIR MUIR

Kylie Minogue with dancers from Rambert Dance Company in Rafael Bonachela's *21* cheap-as-chips showbiz, pop videos are increasingly being used as a crossover forum for cutting-edge choreographers. Rambert Dance Company's Rafael Bonachela spun the wheel full circle by creating the moves for Kylie Minogue's *Love At First Sight*, a favour the Aussie pop diva returned by appearing (on film) in Bonachela's *21* for Rambert.

The Global Showreel

It's no wonder that choreographers, frustrated by the lack of live opportunities for dance, are pouring their creativity into a form that will be seen by millions on a global scale. For many, the video can be used as a showreel which feeds back into finding opportunities for live performance. One of the first to recognise this was French choreographer Philippe Decouflé, whose seminal video for New Order's *True Faith* gave his bouncy talents a major leg up the dance ladder.

Decouflé went on to create the spectacular opening ceremony for the Albertville Winter Olympics in 1992, a ceremony that's set the benchmark for each subsequent event. And with his company DCA, Decouflé has become one of the most sought-after names on the world dance circuit. [DCA is featured in the 2004 edition of Dance Umbrella.] Yet without the platform his madcap bouncy figures found in *True Faith*, Decouflé's star may not have risen so quickly.

What drives the pop video on fast forward is its role in keeping one step ahead of the chart game. From hip-hop gods Outkast to pop divas Britney Spears and Christina Aguilera, a host of artists have been as defined by their dance image as they are by their music style. It's all in the way they move.

There's no denying the dynamic excitement that can erupt when a choreographer gets to work with live musicians on stage. Of course, the whole thing can fall apart, but when it works it creates an unbeatable buzz. Here are some of the best:

Michael Clark / The Fall
I Am Curious, Orange, 1988
T Rex, PJ Harvey and the unforgettable ahead-of-their-time mixes by Jeffrey Hinton have provided Clark with recorded dynamite, but the collision of his spikily beautiful dance steps with the belligerent guitars and mouthy attitude of Mark E. Smith and The Fall was the body electric.

Wim Vandekeybus & Ultima Vez / Woven Hand
Blush, 2003
Belgium's prince of Euro-crash colliding with the solemn gothic beauty of Colorado alternative country rocker David Eugene Edwards and his band was an inspired experiment. Bill Withers' *Ain't No Sunshine* has never sounded – or looked – so deliciously doom laden.

Shobana Jeyasingh / The Balanescu Quartet
Configurations, 1988
Driven by Michael Nyman's pulsating rhythms, Jeyasingh's modern British take on classical Indian dance took geometric flight like string-driven dervishes.

David Bowie / Lindsay Kemp
The Rise and Fall of Ziggy Stardust, 1972
The rock dance spectacular to beat them all, Kemp's bug-like army of scurrying dancers gave the perfect alien edge to Bowie's seminal rock star sci-fi fantasy. Unforgettable.

DANCE LAUGHS

Dance hasn't got a reputation for being a barrel of laughs and, it's true, there aren't many giggles to be had from the lycra-clad navel-gazing brigade. But dance has enormous comedy potential – and some star comedy performers.

Nigel Charnock
Whether in his DV8 days, or working solo (as in the aptly-named *Frank*) or latterly with Helsinki City Dance Theatre, the psychotically witty Charnock has mined a rich vein of humour from his tales of broken hearts, unrequited lust and the sheer damn insanity of it all.

Protein
In *Portrait with Group and Duck*, *Publife* and *The Banquet*, Luca Silvestrini and Bettina Strickler have shot to the top of British (OK, so one's Italian and the other's Swiss) dance with their off-kilter humour and madcap inventiveness. *Publife*, an uproarious slice of boozed-up soap opera, is always staged in an actual pub.

Wendy Houstoun
Nigel Charnock's one-time partner in laughter crimes, Houstoun is a wickedly sharp performer whose self-deprecating wit disguises a steely strength of spirit. Her solo venture *The 48 Almost Love Lyrics* is a great example of the barbed beauties of her work.

HERRINGBONE DESIGN

Madame Galina

New Art Club

For Tom Roden and Peter Shenton, nothing in dance is sacred. Witness *This Is Modern*, an hour-plus of words and motion which are as instructive as they are irreverent. Their brand of dance satire is spot-on, and you don't even need to know all the references to get the gags.

Matthew Bourne

The enormous popular success of Bourne's work, from early ballet parody *Spitfire* to the stylish smash *Play Without Words*, is down in no small part to the sly and sophisticated wit that's seamlessly stitched into his dance works. Bourne just can't take himself seriously, and that's his greatest strength.

Les Ballets Trocadero de Monte Carlo

Old-school comedy it may be, but these butch ballet mickey-takers are surprisingly agile and accomplished technicians. Delighting in names like Galina Getyerlegova, The Trocks would have boxed our ears if we'd left 'em out.

ralf ralf

The Summit is Jonathan and Barnaby Stone's still-timely comedy classic, a sharp skewering of modern-day politics in which public debate is reduced to body language and nonsense sounds. Good news: after too long a hiatus, the siblings are cooking up new work.

Madame Galina

This oversized mock-Russian ballerina (Iestyn Edwards) fabricates lovingly tart send-ups of classical technique, diva-style celebrity and all the attendant pretensions.

TOP POP DANCE PROMOS

A random shuffle through the pop video jukebox

Michael Jackson
Thriller / Beat It (1983)

Often imitated but never bettered, Michael Jackson is the Fred Astaire of the MTV generation. Mannered his crotch-grabbing moves certainly are, but with the ground-breaking theatrics of *Thriller* and the highly choreographed group dynamics of *Beat It*, Jacko's superslick routines are classics of their kind.

Adam & The Ants
Prince Charming (1981)

Adam Ant wasn't really a dancer, but he knew how to move. New Romance, glamour, posing – it's all here, in a kitsch style that Duran Duran, who followed, took to exotic levels.

Kate Bush
Sat In Your Lap (1981)

A major dance fan and idiosyncratic mover, Bush enlisted the help of Seventies dance legend Lyndsay Kemp in her early videos. From the wafty and ethereal (*Wow*) to the arthouse frenetic (*Sat In Your Lap*), she is English pop's unsung dancing queen.

Talking Heads
Once in a Lifetime (1981)

The pop video as performance art, with David Byrne showing that – hey – geeks can dance too. Check out the live performance video *Stop Making Sense* for the full picture.

Elton John
I'm Still Standing (1983)
Self-indulgence on a delirious scale, with Elton in his pomp surrounding himself with skimpily clad dancing lads on the French Riviera. An adrenaline rush from start to finish.

Run DMC vs Jason Nevins
It's Like That (1997)
The break-dance duel may have become a cliché – but this chart-topping video brought streetdance off the, er, streets and on to our TVs.

Jamiroquai
Virtual Insanity (1996)
And the furniture dances too. Jay Kay shows us his nifty footwork while ducking and weaving with a light-on-its-feet settee.

The Featherstonehaughs Draw on The Sketchbooks of Egon Schiele (1997) choreographed by Lea Anderson

Britney Spears
Hit Me Baby One More Time (1999)
Mix together a schoolgirl outfit and a high-kicking spin on the cheerleader routine and what have you got? Global domination. The recent chart-topping *Toxic*, a masterpiece of choreographed cleavage in a trolley-dolly cossie, reveals just how much Britney has grown up.

Sophie Ellis-Bextor
Murder on the Dancefloor (2002)
Come Dancing meets *Strictly Ballroom* as dancehall diva Sophie E-B stilettos the opposition in a cut-throat dance contest. Stomp those feet, girl.

Beyoncé
Crazy In Love (2003)
The bootylicious rumpshaker to beat them all, Beyoncé Knowles doesn't just do it on video. Her live shows reveal she cuts a mean move onstage as well.

Will Young
Your Game (2004)
A stylish homage to Baz Luhrmann's *Moulin Rouge* that curiously evokes Matthew Bourne's *Play Without Words*, this is dance video taken to sophisticated heights.

Dance in Sport

Sport and dance have more in common than the macho brigade care to admit. From the highly choreographed ring antics of body-slamming wrestlers and the magical footwork of boxers from Muhammad Ali to Prince Naseem, all the way through to the more obvious ice-rink artistry of Torvill and

Dean, and the air-splitting arc of the high-board diver, the unity of physical movement required by both disciplines makes them kindred spirits.

When sport hits the heights it can touch all your emotions, making the soul soar with its beauty and stimulating the brain with the marriage of technique and aesthetics. Just picture Thierry Henry twinkle-toeing his way through Premiership defences or Justine Henin-Hardenne floating into another rapier-like backhand. Isn't dance supposed to get you like that?

Given the obvious physical crossover between the two disciplines, choreographers have been fairly slow off the mark to get to grips with the potential. Glen Tetley used t'ai chi for the influential *Embrace Tiger and Return to Mountain*, and Christopher Dean reinvented Christopher Bruce's *Ghost Dances* on ice for protégés the Duchesnays in the early Nineties. But it's only in the past decade that major moves have been made.

Back in the mid-1970s Twyla Tharp was the first choreographer to work with Olympic champion John Curry, who went on to launch his Theatre of Skating. She also choreographed a TV special for ballet dancer Peter Martins and American football players, *Dance is a Man's Sport Too*, in 1980.

Sportorama

One interesting experiment was Lea Anderson's *Sportorama*, a mass-participation event at the Crystal Palace sports complex in London (1999). Aiming to underscore the similarities between the two fields by placing familiar sporting images in a choreographic context, Anderson assembled no less than 120 young sports performers in a site-specific dance project akin to a military operation. She'd tried out the same format in Leicester with *Opéra sportif* in 1991.

Filled with neat ideas, such as mixing-and-matching sporting outfits with events (martial artists in cricket whites, trampolinists in swimming trunks), *Sportorama* was never quite more than the sum of its parts, but it did a fine job in pointing up how close many dance and sport moves are.

Footballet

Performers such as Laurie Booth and, more recently, Russell Maliphant, have drawn on a liquid mixture of gymnastics and martial arts (the Brazilian style of capoeira is a big influence) to help forge their individual movement style. But the most strikingly populist sport-dance has to be *A Dance Tribute to the Art of Football* from Norway's Jo Stromgren Company, a piece still scoring away-wins around Europe some six years after it kicked off.

Swerving neatly clear of too-obvious footie images, Stromgren's love for the beautiful game shines through in a humorous selection of well-thought-out set-pieces. Like all the best ideas, it's hard to believe no one has come up with it before, for football is blessed with the full array of choreographed moves – just check out players lining up for a free kick – and Stromgren dribbles through them in a hymn to testosterone-fuelled action. From the pre-game warm-up through to the post-match shower, Stromgren evokes soccer rituals in a way both fans and non-believers can relate to.

While we wait for an English choreographer to come up with a similarly inspired paean to the rucks and mauls of rugby, honourable mention should be go to *Microphobia* (2004), where Luca Silvestrini and Bettina Strickler put CandoCo through their Olympian paces, and to the company Nitro, which has recently come up with *Slamdunk*. Set in the world of basketball, this is a hip-hop dance musical by company director Felix Crossand and choreographer Benji Reid.

Sorted

Dance of all sorts

Whether you dance professionally or for pleasure, or simply choose to treat it as a spectator sport, there is a plethora of styles to choose from. Of the handful sampled here, each has its own approach to that basic component of human motion – the foot.

African

Bare feet are the norm for traditional African dancing, but there's plenty of body decoration with dancers sporting elaborate costumes, masks, body paint and even stilts.

Dance was an essential part of worship and celebration in tribal Africa. Movement would be used to directly communicate with the gods, placating or appealing to them. Dance could be used to encourage crops, heal the sick, install a new leader and mark rites of passage in people's lives. Traditional dance doesn't take place on a stage, but is something that the whole community takes part in. Each dance has a particular meaning or story to tell.

There are a huge number of different dances and styles across the continent, but they are all strongly tied to music and the intricate polyrhythms that are the basis of African music. The interplay of those multilayered rhythms is reflected in the movements of the body, where strong stamping feet underpin undulating torsos.

Elements of African music and dance have influenced numerous other dance styles including jazz, tap and salsa, reggae and dancehall. The hit West End show *Umoja* celebrates the music and dance of South Africa. Adzido Pan African Dance Ensemble tour productions based on traditional dance, while other UK-based companies such as Sakoba Dance Theatre, Badejo Arts and Irie! Dance Theatre fuse African dance with contemporary dance and street styles. Soweto-born dancer Vincent Sekwati Mantsoe tours widely, performing intense solo pieces that commune with the spirits of his Zulu ancestors.

> **"** In the black heritage we have our own *Giselles* and *Swan Lakes*," says Vincent Sekwati Mantsoe. "These are important stories of our lives. I have my own way of telling stories. But I have to make them so people can really understand, and not be puzzled or frustrated. My work is based on the rituals and spirits of my ancestors. You're not allowed to do sacred dances or go into a trance onstage, but I know how to control myself. The audience should be able to come with me on a journey and see the spirits I'm seeing.
>
> "My background is very spiritual," he continues. "My mother is a sangoma, what you would call a traditional healer. When I grew up I encouraged myself to respect each and every culture. I think I have a reason to be here in life, to send a message to all kinds of cultures. I've managed to incorporate traditional dances from many different cultures into my work. I've borrowed from Japanese and Chinese, Balinese, Aboriginals, West Africa. I never once had a thought that I'm doing something wrong. **"**

Ballet

Aside from tutus, pointe shoes are the most recognisable symbol of ballet. The satin slippers have leather soles and toes hardened with a special glue to make them stiff enough to stand on the tip. Dancers darn toes of their shoes or sometimes cut away the fabric so that they don't slip. The pointe shoe allows female dancers to look as if they're walking on air by elongating the lines of their bodies. In the 1830s Marie Taglioni garnered huge celebrity for her delicate pointe work, an embodiment of the sylphlike ethereality of the nineteenth-century ballerina. Men have occasionally danced on pointe, but mainly for comic effect. The best example is Les Ballets Trockadero de Monte Carlo, an American group popularly known as The Trocks. In their devoted spoofs of classical ballet and contemporary dance, all female roles are danced – and quite well even when on pointe – by men.

Classical ballet originated in the Italian and French courts in the late sixteenth century, the preserve of aristocratic amateurs who liked to indulge in lavish allegorical spectacles in honour of the monarchy. The first ballet academy was founded in Paris in 1661 by Louis XIV, himself an avid dance fan. Over the next three hundred years a strict and detailed technique developed there and spread to other European capitals.

Ballet is based on five positions of the feet, and recognisable steps include the arabesque (where one leg is lifted straight behind the body) and the pirouette (a turn on one foot or toe). A key element is turn out, where the toes and knees point outwards rather than straight forward. This was originally a way for aristocratic performers to show off their elegant calves and heeled shoes, but it also enables dancers to lift their legs much higher than they could otherwise – hence the ear-brushing extensions of such dancers of today as superstar Sylvie Guillem and George Piper Dances' Oxana Panchenko.

Flamenco

Firecracker footwork is the trademark of flamenco dance. Performers gain extra explosiveness by wearing shoes or boots with nails driven into the heels, which also help the shoes to grip the floor.

Flamenco with Juana Jiménez

Flamenco originated as a gypsy dance of Andalusia, in southern Spain, with Arabic and Moorish influences. The root of the dance is flamenco song, or cante. It tells mournful tales of joy, love, pain and despair. Early flamenco was danced with an accompaniment of only singing and clapping. Even then the rhythmic foot stamping which the dance is so known for was an essential part of the musical interplay. Flamenco guitar has since become a solo instrument in its own right.

A dancer will improvise on the rhythms of flamenco songs, creating a rhythmic dialogue with the musicians or other dancers. This makes all flamenco dancers choreographers too. The frenzied footwork is balanced by a proud arched back and elegant arm movements which snake across the body. Flamenco is a passionate and spontaneous art. It can feel like a flirtation, a confrontation or a duel between two dancers, or an intense personal journey. At the heart of flamenco is "duende", a word sometimes translated as a soulful longing. It signifies an emotional depth reached through music, dance and song.

Andalusians can be seen dancing flamenco in bars and at festivals, where flamenco is more a way of life than a set of steps. Professional dancers tend to fall into two camps. Flamenco puro, the traditionalists, are exemplified by Antonio Montoya, "El Farruco", and his grandson Juan Manuel Fernandez, "Farruquito". Modernisers like Eva Yerbabuena and Maria Pages bring in elements of theatre, narrative and other dance influences. Flamenco's most famous current exponent is Joaquín Cortés, the creator of glitzy spectacles combining blazing technique with narcissistic glamour.

South Asian

Ghungroos (ankle bells) provide jangling percussion to classical Indian dancers' feet. A dominant form is bharata natyam, a South Indian temple dance that may have developed more than 3000 years ago. Unlike ballet, where the dancer tries to escape gravity, in Indian dance the feet are solidly rooted to the earth while hands and arms are intricately deployed and the face is exceptionally expressive.

Bharata natyam is based on three principles: natya (story-telling), nritta (rhythm) and nritya (expression). As a form of religious worship, dancers would invoke deities and tell stories of the gods. In the early nineteenth century, the movement was codified by a group of brothers, the Tanjore Quartet. There are 108 karanas (units of movement) which each have a specific meaning, including thirteen head gestures, 36 glances, seven movements of the eyeballs, nine for the eyelids and 67 for the hands. Bharata natyam is traditionally performed by women.

Kathak, a North Indian form, is usually danced by men. Nobody knows the exact origins of kathak dance. Nurtured in the Hindu temples and village squares of northern India, it was performed by an itinerant community of storytellers. Their subjects were epic mythological and moral tales, usually with a devotional slant.

During the period of Muslim rule, dancers imported from Persia fell in love with kathak, helping to secularize it and carry it into the royal courts. The ensuing patronage of kings and emperors both freed and polished it into a sophisticated art, notable for its lightning-fast pirouettes, stamping feet and statuesque poses.

Birmingham-based choreographer Nahid Siddiqui is one of contemporary Britain's best kathak practitioners. "The most natural of all the Indian dance forms," she calls it, "and the one with the greatest similarity to ballet. Dancing it, one is grounded and elevated at the same time."

Traditional Indian dance in its various guises is popular today in Britain. As a reflection of their diverse heritage and influences, a number of choreographers push the envelope by combining dance styles. Shobana Jeyasingh is a seminal figure. This Madras-born choreographer has devised her own hybrid blend of bharata natyam-flecked contemporary movement. Akram Khan is a classically trained kathak dancer whose choreography is what he calls "a confusion" of styles.

Irish

An Irish dancer's feet move so fast it might be hard to see what they're clad in, but there are three types of shoes worn for Irish step dancing. Hard shoes, for hornpipes and jigs, are similar to a tap shoe and perfect for the percussive steps that dominate Irish dance onstage. The shoes have a heel which can be hollow for a sharper sound, and a hard "tip" on the ball of the shoe, made from fibreglass or metal, which may have a flattened front edge for showy steps like toe stands. For dancing reels, light jigs and slipjigs girls wear soft leather pumps, with criss-cross laces called ghillies. Men's reel shoes are similar to hard shoes but without the tips.

Irish step dancing (so called because eight bars of music make a "step") is very distinctive in style. The dancer's body is kept still and upright, with hands by the sides. The feet provide all the action. Quick, complex footwork peppered with flying leaps complements the rhythms of Irish folk music. Early competitions saw dancers performing on table tops or atop a barrel, but modern dancers tend to stick to the stage.

Irish dancing as we know it developed in the eighteenth and nineteenth centuries under the tutelage of dancing masters who toured towns and villages teaching jigs and reels, elaborating on centuries-old dances. Step dancing was enthusiastically promoted following the independence of the

Republic in 1921, both in Ireland itself and in America where Irish immigrants proudly preserved their heritage.

One such Irish-American, Chicago-born Michael Flatley, could be held responsible for the huge mainstream explosion in Irish dancing during the Nineties. A former World Irish Dancing Champion, Flatley and his partner Jean Butler performed at the 1994 Eurovision Song Contest in *Riverdance*. The show, a grand piece of populist cultural heritage, became a worldwide phenomenon. Flatley brought panache and showmanship to the form, and later starred in his own extravaganza *Lord of the Dance*.

Jazz

Soft leather shoes with a rubber sole are perfect for the dancing that's most associated with bright lights and Broadway. Think the kids from *Fame*. Think *Chicago* and *All That Jazz*.

Like tap, jazz came out of the black American community and was based on African and jazz rhythms. Jazz music was big on the dancefloors in the dance-crazy 1920s and 30s, with dances such as the cakewalk, the Charleston and the jitterbug catching on big. After jazz dance shifted into show business it never looked back. In the 1950s it became the dominant form on Broadway, while from the 1960s teacher-choreographers like Matt Mattox and Luigi expanded its vocabulary.

Bob Fosse is one of the key names in show-stopping jazz dance, steering it into a cutting, thrusting and scintillating direction all his own. He choreographed a slew of stage musicals and a handful of films including Broadway's original *Chicago*, the Oscar-winning big-screen version of *Cabaret* and the dazzling autobiographical *All That Jazz*.

Jerome Robbins used expressive jazz moves in *West Side Story* and *New York Export: Opus Jazz*. Alvin Ailey was also influenced by the form. Ballet Jazz de Montreal is Canada's top jazz dance troupe, while Sheron Wray's JazzXchange leads the UK pack. London's JazzCotech and the Jiving Lindy Hoppers have heralded a resurgence in the "old skool" style. Traces of jazz can even be found in Union Dance's eclectic brew of contemporary, street and martial arts moves.

Street Dance

For Run DMC it was unlaced Adidas. Whatever your brand of choice, trainers are essential footwear for budding b-boys and girls and their ilk. Street dance is a fairly loose term for what they do, encompassing funk dance, breakdancing and pop dance. At the heart of it is hip-hop, as much of a philosophy as an often hugely commercialised music/dance/cultural genre.

Dance-wise it all started at New York block parties in the early Seventies, where Kool DJ Herc noticed that the dancers loved the drum breaks in his funk records. He bought two copies of the same record and mixed them in a way that extended the break for the dancers: breakdancing. He also came up with the term b-boy, which, depending on who you consult, means break boy, boogie boy, beat boy or Bronx boy.

Crews like the Zulu Kings and Dynamite Rockers would battle for street supremacy, with "uprockin" fighting moves

> **"** Hip-hoppers are very informed people," Robert Hylton says. "We borrow from all cultures. But you have to understand what you're borrowing, or else you're just stealing. I've never made the decision yet to strip my dance down to one form. You have to create an individual style. That's what I pursue, whether on the street or the stage. **"**

countered by "downrockin" – when the dancer takes his weight on his hand and weaves fast footwork around it. Later West Coast styles like locking, popping and boogaloo caught on, especially after Michael Jackson went robotic while singing *Dancin' Machine* on national TV. (He lifted the moonwalk, or backslide, from The Electric Boogaloos.) The moves got gradually more acrobatic, with Crazy Legs and Frosty Freeze from the Rock Steady Crew showing off their

Jonzi D (Still Brock Productions)

backspins, headspins, windmills and the suicide (a front flip landing flat on your back) in New York's Central Park.

Breaking went truly mainstream, and global, in the 1980s. After a dip in popularity there's been a steady revival in interest, with hip-hop jams at clubs and festivals across the UK and Europe. Hip-hop has featured in major stage shows like *Jam on the Groove* and *Bounce*. Pioneering US hip-hop choreographer Rennie Harris blends his chosen genre and theatre to stand-out effect. Harris's *Rome & Jewels* is an especially strong riff on Shakespeare's star-cross'd lovers, its real focus being the masochistic impulses inside black urban male machismo.

British artists like performer and director Jonzi D, body-popping poet Benji Reid and Robert Hylton are in the forefront of hip-hop innovation. The latter dubs his original blend of street, contemporary, jazz and ballet vocabularies Urban Classicism. Other hip-hop dance notables include the French-Algerian Compagnie Kafig, former Twyla Tharp dancer Victor Quijada's Canadian troupe Rubberbandance Group, and Tommy the Clown, star of LA's underground hip-hop clowning movement known as Krumping.

Tango

Sexy heels are essential for any woman who wants to tango – and a sexy partner is a bonus. This seductive dance grew out of the slums and dance halls of Buenos Aires in the 1880s, where Spanish settlers mixed with locals and immigrants from around the world. Tango later crossed the Atlantic to become a big hit in Europe in the 1920s and 30s, partly thanks to the endorsement of suave cinema idol Rudolph Valentino. As with most social dances, the music is integral to the dance. Tango's slow 2/4 pulse, rhythmic melody and the distinctive sound of the bandoneon (an Argentinian accordion) are easily recognisable. Accomplished dancers, however, never move to a strict beat, but rather follow the phrase of the melody.

In the early days men would often tango together, but the moves came into their own as a slow, sensual duet between lovers. The dance is improvised based on a number of basic steps, often embellished with a flirtatious flick of the foot or a sultry slide of the toe up your partner's thigh. The male partner always leads, deciding where to go next and signalling to his partner with his head or a subtle hand movement on her back.

While still danced in ballrooms, tango can also be seen in slickly choreographed shows on stages around the world featuring stylised ensemble pieces as well as more intimate duets. Al Pacino danced it in *Scent of a Woman*, and Madonna and Antonio Banderas tangoed in *Evita*. Many choreographers have drawn upon elements of tango, including Frederick Ashton in *Façade* and the recent contemporary works of Richard Alston and Henri Oguike. But apart from bona fide tango dancers, nobody has gotten as much erotic mileage out of the form as veteran American dance-maker Paul Taylor in his steamy *Piazzolla Caldera*.

Tap

The right shoes are instrumental, literally, in the success of a twinkle-toed tap dancer. Tap shoes have aluminium plates, or cleats, attached at the toe and heel which can be adjusted, tighter or looser, to make the desired sound. Although this style of tap shoe is standard today, the first tappers actually danced in wooden-soled clogs; metal taps weren't used until after the 1920s.

Tap dancing is seen as an all-American dance form, but its origins lie in a combination of Irish clogging, African dance and drumming rhythms, all thrown into the melting pot of mid-nineteenth century America. You could catch the likes of William Henry "Juba" Lane and, later, Bill "Bojangles" Robinson in vaudeville clubs and minstrel shows, or on street corners where dancers would jam, like musicians, beating out complex syncopated rhythms and trading fours – taking turns, each trying to outdo the others' previous improvised displays.

There are a small number of basic tap steps – shuffle, hop, step, tap, ball change – plus an infinite number of combinations. From its improvisatory roots tap jumped onto influences from social dances and jazz dance and, in the process, became a more stylised, choreographed form. It hit the big time in the 1920s and 30s in top speakeasies like The Cotton Club in Harlem and on the Broadway stage. Tap also featured in the earliest Hollywood musicals. Racial politics denied black dancers much significant screen time. It was their white counterparts (or imitators) like Fred Astaire and Gene Kelly who became (deserved) popular legends.

Stage shows keep the tap flame burning. In the 1992 musical *Crazy For You*, Broadway choreographer Susan Stroman went to town on a hotly percussive production number to the song *I Got Rhythm*. Stephen Mear achieved similar glories via

In *Backstage on Broadway: Musicals and Their Makers*, author Marty Bell hangs out in the studio with choreographer Susan Stroman as she devises moves for the musical *Crazy For You*. Sitting on a folding chair to put on her beat-up, high-heeled green tap shoes, Stroman remarks, "People like to use the same tap shoes for years. You change the taps, but the leather gets soft and moulds to your feet." But her assistant Chris Peterson contradicts that view. "I keep my taps even if I change my shoes. They're worn down and give you that thin sound you want. I don't like those heavy Capezio taps. The sound is so clunky."

a huge tap number in the recent West End hit *Anything Goes*. *Tap Dogs*, by Australian former steel worker Dein Perry, put a laddishly modern spin on that old shuffle, hop, step, while *Stomp* found rhythm in everyday items like garbage lids and plastic bags. But the most sustained feat of contemporary tapping was probably *Bring in Da Noise, Bring in Da Funk*, purist tap sensation Savion Glover's history of black America and its dances.

Compañia Tango X2 – Artistic Director
Miguel Angel Zotto and Soledad Ribero

Motion History

Sweet inspiration

The truth, it's said, is seldom pure and never simple. And so it is with the inspiration for dance. You might sometimes hear the term "pure dance", meaning abstract dance, movement for movement's sake rather than movement as vehicle for a story. But it's rare to find dance that can disclaim all influence from music, costume, stage settings or thematic material of any kind.

Some would argue that dance can never be entirely abstract however hard it tries. Since movement is performed by men and women it inevitably evokes some kind of "story" about human experience, and some flicker of recognition in those watching. We human beings, after all, start learning to read body language in the cradle. We also learn very quickly that meaning is subject to context. Eloquent as some physical actions might be, they are never literal statements of fact or emotion. That raised arm – is it raised in anger, in greeting or in fear? These things are open to nuance and interpretation. And how an audience reads the movement in dance can't help but be influenced by the sounds, colours, textures and allusions that accompany them onstage.

In Context

From the earliest court ballets of the seventeenth century to today's contemporary dance, choreographers have sought out

SCULPTED, PAINTED, DRAWN

A river ran through the dance performance *La Danse du Temps*, but not one that was likely to flood or even dampen the stage. That's because the river in this collaboration between French choreographer Regine Chopinot and British sculptor Andy Goldsworthy was metaphorical.

The title, which translates as *The Dance of Time*, was a tip-off. The work conveyed themes of passage, flow and change in several ways. One was the fact of human ageing. The cast of sixteen ranged in age from mid-twenties to mid-seventies. Stretching the age barrier in a notoriously youth-oriented art form like dance is one thing. Goldsworthy's participation plunged Chopinot into deeper conceptual waters.

Using materials like stone, wood, earth and ice, the artist has gained worldwide fame for his ingenious investigations into nature's cyclical patterns. In *La Danse*, the backdrop was the continuous projection of a time-lapse film of one of Goldsworthy's indoor installations. Scottish clay was packed onto a wall-frame in Digne, France. In performance the clay cracked as it dried and, almost imperceptibly, a serpentine form emerged. Goldsworthy's work is called, aptly, *The River*.

The notion of different worlds colliding is one of the most intriguing features of art/dance collaborations. As American choreographer Stephen Petronio recognised, "It's a fragile relationship. One involves lots of money, the other doesn't. One is object-oriented, the other ephemeral." In the 1999 dance *Strange Attractors*, Petronio's company shared space with two large,

suppliers of context. Where once they chose principally composers and painters, more recently they have invited video and lighting artists as well as fashion designers in on the act, shaping, guiding and colouring the movement they invent.

reflective discs by Anish Kapoor. "A sculpture onstage dictates a certain approach," Petronio remarked soon after its premiere. "Anish has given me something changing and alive, more about light and movement than the objects themselves."

Earlier examples of the art/dance interface abound, from Diaghilev's recruitment of Picasso and Matisse for his Ballets Russes, to Martha Graham's reliance on Isamu Noguchi, to Merce Cunningham's ventures with Robert Rauschenberg, Jasper Johns and Andy Warhol. In Britain, think Richard Alston and Howard Hodgkin, Ashley Page and Bruce McLean, or Patrick Caulfield's redesigns of Frederick Ashton's *Rhapsody*.

Trisha Brown, America's post-modern dance diva, is articulate about collaboration's pleasures and pitfalls, having worked with the likes of Nancy Graves and Donald Judd. A trilogy of jazz-based dances, inspired by the music of trumpeter-composer Dave Douglas, featured designs by painter Terry Winters.

"With the exception of Bob Rauschenberg, who is a master in the theatre, collaborating is a crap shoot," Brown says. "You see, I'm bringing artists who are at the top of their field into unfamiliar circumstances and teaching them as fast as I can about the intricacies of the theatre. We work in parallel tracks, figuring out what kind of relationship we're headed towards. What I get in the end is a comrade with whom I am discussing the development of my work, which is very important to have. Finally, one way or another, each of these very independent, very skilled, very, very extraordinary artists and I carve up the culture."

Together they have found inspiration in subject matter ranging from make-believe (*Swan Lake*) to gender politics (Lloyd Newson's work for DV8). They have adapted existing stories from Chekhov to the *Arabian Nights*. They have risen to the challenge of gallery art (an Anish Kapoor sculpture, say) and explored the possibilities of raw materials that in themselves seem quite mundane. A contemporary company from Southeast Asia developed a piece performed on a stage covered in mounds of rice grains through which the dancers slowly carved paths, adapting their movement to the task. Other choreographers have stretched the body's natural limits using artificial limbs or mountaineering equipment.

Make Mine Music

But without doubt the biggest influence on choreography past and present has been music. The American Mark Morris once said that one of the reasons he makes dance is "to trick people into hearing music better". You don't need to be a critic or dance aficionado to recognise that whether the dance is set to a Thai pop song or a Gershwin piano piece, Italian madrigals or

METAPOLIS – project 972, Frédéric Flamand/Zaha Hadid
Charleroi/Danses – Plan K

rock'n'roll, the Morris piece you're watching is a direct physical translation of what you're hearing. This is not a new idea. The founder of American ballet, Russian-born George Balanchine, was juggling with a similar sensual/cerebral equation half a century earlier, devising new twists on old steps to match the jagged patterns of Igor Stravinsky's music, itself a lively amalgam of rooted tradition and New World drive. Often the design influences in the Balanchine/Stravinsky ballets were kept to a minimum. The backdrop was plain blue, the dancers wore practice leotards. As a contemporary observed, "You see the music and you hear the dance." The choreographer was determined that nothing should get in the way of that.

What's On First?

One of the questions uppermost in people's minds when wondering how traditional ballets are put together is "What comes first, the music or the steps?" In cases where a choreographer has chosen to "set" movement to an existing score, the answer is obvious. Though it might sound as if Frederick Ashton asked Franz Liszt to compose him a piano piece featuring the cough of a consumptive courtesan for his 1963 ballet *Marguerite and Armand*, we know that he couldn't have because the Liszt Sonata was written a hundred years earlier. The bewitching confluence of story and sound is the result of an astute choreographer spotting material perfectly shaped to his theme, and then following its shapes and textures down to the very last crotchet.

Waking Beauty

The answer is less clear-cut when the music is more or less contemporary with the steps. Take the Tchaikovsky ballets of the 1890s. The greatest of these marked the first true collaboration between a dance-maker and a composer. It came about, oddly enough, because of an earlier flop. *Swan Lake*, on its first showing, was what box-office managers call a stinker. The chief gripe of Russian audiences was that Tchaikovsky's score, with its highly organised key structure underpinning the story, was "too symphonic" and that the music overwhelmed the dance. Those who'd come for fancy decor and pretty sounds found their emotions stirred more

SHEDDING LIGHT

Lighting seems the most obvious element of a live dance performance. Without it, how would we ever see what's going on? Yet if that were all lighting is about, there'd be no need for anything more than glaring worklights to illuminate a playing area. In some cases it's meant to support a work without calling attention to itself. Others prefer to treat it as a major creative element. For them lighting conjures atmosphere out of the air. It paints moods. It defines space and sculpts bodies.

The best lighting designers offer no push-button theories or formulas for their branch of stage magic, which is to provide the environment in which a dance exists. Finland's Mikki Kunttu, who regularly collaborates with dance-making fellow countryman Tero Saarinen, believes light can create three-dimensional illusions by suggesting intimate proximity or unfathomable distance. In performance the lighting is so integral, Saarinen says, "it's like Mikki's dancing with us."

Lighting may coincide with or contradict physical rhythms, and emphasise or downplay an onstage psychological relationship. As Michael Hulls and choreographer Russell Maliphant use it, or Guy Hoare working with Henri Oguike, light can even determine choreographic structure.

Despite an engineering background, designer Michael Mannion always had a leaning towards dance; he even studied than they'd bargained for. Rather than bowing to this rather depressing complaint, the director of the Imperial Theatres realised that the way forward lay in encouraging communication. Great composers and great choreographers could indeed meet on equal terms, but first they must sit round a table and talk about it, heading towards the grand intended result together instead of holing up in their separate ivory towers and complaining that the other had got it wrong.

dance diva Martha Graham's technique. Lighting, he says, "can ruin or help a dance. It can also take the choreography somewhere it couldn't go alone. For some shows I think, 'I'm going to do everything I can to be noticed.' On others I'm trying to convince a choreographer, this'll work." His approach varies depending on with whom he's collaborating. "Javier De Frutos has been exacting from the start. He architecturally marks out the space with dotted lines – long corridors coming off circles. With Mark Baldwin I nearly always have to describe colours."

In Lucy Carter's opinion, talking about light is pretty unsatisfactory. "Until you actually see it, you don't know what it's going to be." Aside from fruitful associations with Charles Linehan and Shobana Jeyasingh, Wayne McGregor has been Carter's main collaborator. She's lit more than twenty of his dances. "We work quite graphically," she says, "because his ideas are technology-led." How ironic, then, is Carter's admission that she doesn't keep abreast of all the latest technology. "I don't see lighting as a technical thing," she explains. "I ignore that side until I have my ideas and concepts." Crucially, Lucy Carter says, "Light is emotive. And it directs the audience's view." And the ways we feel about and respond to dance.

That's how Tchaikovsky produced the score for *The Sleeping Beauty*, and St Petersburg's venerable ballet master Marius Petipa made dance to fit it. But instead of the choreographer demanding swingeing cuts and alterations once the music was written, Petipa discussed the ballet's outline with Tchaikovsky tactfully in advance, suggesting time signatures for each section, how many bars each would require, even dropping hints about how each section might sound. It was the first true collaboration between dance and music, and many still think *The Sleeping Beauty* score is the greatest ever written for dance.

Equal Partners

It was another son of St Petersburg who took the idea one giant leap further. Sergei Diaghilev was neither a choreographer nor a musician. In fact, he was a law student when he first joined the city's arty social set at the turn of the twentieth century. But he was also a magnet for talent, and organising a Russian art exhibition in Paris soon led to exporting opera and ballet there too. By 1909 he had gathered an ad hoc touring company that included Russia's finest young dancers, and a repertoire anchored by the radical new choreography of Mikhail Fokine.

Fokine was so ticked off about the rut ballet was in that he wrote to *The Times* setting out a five-point plan to rescue it. Among various pleas for dance to be less formulaic, his Aim No. 5 was that dance, music and design should be equal partners, each reflecting the dance's subject matter, setting and historical period. That might not sound remotely revolutionary now, but it raised enough hackles in 1909 for Fokine to flee Russia and join Diaghilev's Ballets Russes in Paris. There he could put his reforms into practice.

Puppet On Strings

Petrushka (1911) was the great collaboration that followed, with choreography by Fokine, designs and libretto (or story) by the painter Alexandre Benois, and music by the young Igor Stravinsky, another of Diaghilev's finds. It was a hot ticket. Every element in *Petrushka* broke new ground. The libretto was novel because it dealt not with gods or royalty or even creatures from legend, but with ordinary people enjoying the sights at a fair. The music was astonishingly fresh in the way it captured the aural impressions of the fairground, switching suddenly mid-tune to a snatch of something else, sometimes melding all these sensations together.

The metre of the music, as well as its rhythm, was complex and forever changing, which in turn affected Fokine's choreography. This bore out all his ideas about the need for suiting movement material to theme. In *Petrushka*, each character or group of characters has their own dance style: a chorus of Russian peasant women perform folk dances, a pair of competing street dancers pirouette on pointe, the marionettes in a puppet show move according to their type (a floppy rag pierrot, a pert girl doll and a stiffly jointed soldier doll). There's even a dancing bear.

Rite Or Right?

A mere two years later, *The Rite of Spring* (*Le Sacre du printemps*) threw the rulebook in the air once more. Diaghilev was again the kingpin, but this time he brought the experimental genius of Stravinsky into explosive contact with one of the company's star dancers, Vaslav Nijinsky. As a budding choreographer, Nijinsky's ideas about what kinds of movement might be appropriate to ballet pushed the envelope as never before. Because the steps of *Rite* were never formally written down,

> **❝❝** To me, that music was the original disco. **❞❞**
>
> Dance Theatre of Harlem choreographer Robert Garland on
> *The Rite of Spring*

we can't be sure how it looked. What we do know is those steps turned the old dance rules on their head. *Rite* was a sensationally bold attempt to match the music's clashing colours and barbarous rhythms. Dancers' legs were turned in, with the feet pigeon-toed. They danced with their backs to the audience (an insult never known before), ran in fierce concentric circles or shook as if an earthquake had just struck. The sum effect famously prompted a furore from the first-night audience, not just after the performance but actually during it.

It was all too much. *Rite* was dropped after thirteen showings, though Stravinsky's score went on to acquire the status of a sacred text – and still a virtual rite of passage – for choreographers. More than a hundred dances have been set to it, ranging from a comic-strip-inspired version by the American Paul Taylor (with a narrative hilariously far-removed from the original) and Michael Clark's *Mmm* (1992), also known as *Michael's Modern Masterpiece*, which juxtaposed the original music with punk rock.

Modern Masters

By the time Stravinsky and George Balanchine settled in America, the composer had moved on – to the past. Neoclassicism is the capsule term given to what Stravinsky was doing with music in the 1940s and 50s, and to the dance style that developed in parallel. Both harked back to forms of the past, but simultaneously looked forward with their sleek dynamism, jazzy thrusts and unexpected twists of body logic.

Here the creative process really did happen neck and neck. Often Stravinsky would send single pages of music to Balanchine as he completed them, and the choreographer would wait eagerly for each day's post before working on the next short section of dance.

Martha's Marvels

Diaghilev had introduced dance to the world of fine art, urging a whole generation of serious painters to try their hand at theatre design. But it was the so-called mother of modern dance, Martha Graham, who saw the stage potential of sculpture – how plastic forms, unlike painted sets, might actually be incorporated into the action. Isamu Noguchi, an American of Japanese descent, was her sculptor of choice. He produced designs – often amounting to a single iconic object – for more than twenty Graham dances. While these rarely offered more than a hint of realistic setting, they created a play of lines which echoed the forms of the choreography. Today spectators often find it hard not to smile when they read in the programme that the knobbly prominence forming the centrepiece of *Errand into the Maze* (1947) is "based on a woman's pelvic bone".

Noguchi's designs influenced Graham's dances on a practical level, providing platforms and focal points on and around which the performers could move. On a symbolic level they plugged into the many layers of Graham's mythical themes, giving visual form to Medea's avenging passions or the inward geography of Clytemnestra's heart. Jungian psychology, feminism, Graham's own angular body type and even her disastrous love life had an equally crucial influence on the content of her dance. Fashion too, was seen by Graham as part of dance's remit, and in the latter part of her career, all her stage clothes were designed by Halston.

Cunning Chance

One of the few male dancers in Graham's company in the 1940s was Merce Cunningham, who soon had his own ideas about making dance. He too made choreography out of the way he looked and danced; unlike Graham, he was springy and quick, and trained in ballet. Willingly swayed by the theories of his partner, the composer John Cage, Cunningham's chief inspiration was something much less tangible: the notion of chance. He maintained that dance should reflect the dense information overload that we have to deal with on a daily basis in today's world. Under the influence of modern

Merce Cunningham by Christian Witkin from *Dance 2wice*

art theory, where every form and colour competed equally for the viewer's attention, a typical Cunningham dance had many things happening at once. The choreographer no longer guided the spectator's gaze to the soloist or main event, but left them to choose for themselves where they wanted to look, and when.

Cunningham's dances, unlike Graham's, weren't about struggle, or emotion, or psychology or symbolism. They weren't about anything, he said, except bodies moving "in space and time". But the choreography wasn't – couldn't – be colourless (as we said at the start). It sometimes contained observations of the way people and animals behaved. In a piece called *Beach Birds* the dancers swarm and disperse in the manner of seagulls, and though there is nothing so crude as people pretending to be birds, the allusion is helped along by

CHAPTER 4 • MOTION HISTORY

the costumes: white-and-black leotards that cover their hands and seem to suggest birds' wings.

Whereas virtually every dance made before had been connected, as if by an umbilical cord, to the phrasing of its musical score, Cunningham cut that old connection, adding music only *after* he'd made the dance. And if you're wondering how on earth the dancers kept time, or knew when to start and stop without aural cues, the answer is that Cunningham rehearsed his dancers with a stop watch. Which isn't to say that music doesn't play a part in a Cunningham dance event. It does, but it happens separately, almost as an add-on. Often the dancers don't know what the score will be until the day of the performance, and if you're lucky you can spot them smiling secretly to themselves as they launch into their practised moves and register the spontaneous points of connection – or not – with the unfamiliar sounds.

The accidental quality in Cunningham's dance is deeply embedded in the creative process too. In an early work, *Suite by Chance*, he worked out fifteen different ways of jumping, then tossed a coin to determine how they would be used in the piece. By allowing chance to enter his choreography, he said, he felt "in touch with natural resources far greater than my own personal inventiveness could ever be". In other words, by using random selection processes – dice, the *I Ching*, or later, customized computer software – he believed he could discover combinations of movements he would not have thought of himself.

> ❝ The function of music is to release us from the tyranny of conscious thought. I really like that music does that. It goes down to the gut centre. I think that's where dance comes from, too. ❞
>
> Choreographer Glen Tetley

[h]Interland – 2002 Shobana Jeyasingh Dance Company. Dancers: Mavin Khoo and Sowmya Gopalan.

Songs of the Wanderers performed by Cloud Gate Dance Theatre of Taiwan

CandoCo in Stephen Petronio's *The Human Suite*

Kaash with Akram Kahn

Merce Cunningham Dance Company performing *Anniversary Events* at Tate Modern

Paul Liburd and Amy Hollingsworth of Rambert Dance Company in Wayne McGregor's *PreSentient*

Rota with Companhia de Dança Deborah Colker

Bill T. Jones/Arnie Zane Dance Company

Rooftops and Walls or Over the Top

Between these all-or-nothing schools of influence – between Graham and Cunningham, the twin axes of modern dance – lies a world of infinite variety. The so-called "post-modernists" of the 1960s and 70s rejected the whole idea of dance as specialised movement and made pieces out of running, walking or crawling. Trisha Brown expressed her militancy by taking performance into unexplored places. In *Roof Piece* (1971) she sited her dancers on rooftops over twelve blocks in lower Manhattan and had them relay the movements from one to the next. That same year in *Walking on the Wall* she had her dancers using ropes, pulleys and mountaineering gear to do just what the title describes.

But the styles that choreographers forge for themselves are never set in stone. Only a few years after her "equipment" phase, Trisha Brown was rediscovering what she called "a rapture to move". In 1983 she made the beautiful *Set and Reset*, which subtly referenced her old mode by opening with a dancer apparently walking along the length of the back wall, but opened out into intricately sensuous loping, tumbling, full-on dance. In the 1990s Brown "discovered" music, a thing she had considered an indulgence in her post-modern years, and set about understanding the formal inventiveness of instrumental works such as Bach's *Musical Offering* so that she could craft her dance to match. Having "done" baroque music, she then moved on to jazz.

Pick and Mix

Music and colour, plot, character, set design and lavish dancerliness all became possible again, once dance had got over its puritanical phase. Kenneth MacMillan made the three-act story ballet live again in full-evening works such as *Romeo and*

Juliet, *Manon* and *Mayerling*. Frederick Ashton delved into the dramatic canon with a ravishing *Midsummer Night's Dream* and *A Month in the Country*, based on Turgenev's play. And contemporary dance began soaking up influences from all over. All the old boundaries – geographic and cultural – were flattened in a great global pick-and-mix, as choreographers began surfing the whole world for ideas. Twyla Tharp's *Deuce Coupe*, for example, mixed rock'n'roll dance and ballet steps and set them to songs by the Beach Boys. Mark Morris combined the expressionist gestures of early modern dance with Balkan circle dances in his version of Purcell's *Dido and Aeneas* (campily taking the role of the Queen of Carthage for himself, yet also mining the tragedy in it). Shobana Jeyasingh deconstructed Indian classical dance, commissioning a raft of new music from Western composers in the process. Lloyd Newson based an evening of dance on the story of the mass murderer Denis Nilsen. Matthew Bourne turned ballet in on itself and made revisionist versions of *La Sylphide* (which was set in modern Glasgow and called *Highland Fling*), *The Nutcracker*, and a hugely successful *Swan Lake* with male swans.

Having trawled the world for inspiration, where will choreographers look next? Computer technology offers one way forward – witness the recent work of Merce Cunningham in America and Wayne McGregor in Britain. Russell Maliphant is currently forging a distinctive path with his velvety-tough movement style derived from a knowledge of biodynamics, Rolfing, and Brazilian capoeira. Meanwhile the Philadelphia-based Rennie Harris scored a bull's-eye with a hip-hop treatment of *Romeo and Juliet*, Leeds-based Darshan Singh Bhuller plumbed political depths with a piece about the Balkan conflict, and France-based Angelin Preljocaj makes magic with full-evening works inspired by states of ecstasy and trance. Choreography may be as vulnerable as any art form to the pendulum of fashion, but clearly there's no longer any such thing as "a suitable subject for dance".

DANCE UNDER THE INFLUENCE OF …
COSTUME

Triadic Ballet (1922)
Bauhaus-influenced ballet choreographed and designed by Oskar Schlemmer in which the dancers' geometric costumes resembled cups, saucers, pyramids and other inanimate objects. The costumes have ended up on permanent display in the Stuttgart Museum.

A Tragedy of Fashion (1926)
Witty one-act ballet by Frederick Ashton, his first, which depicts the trials and tribulations of a couturier who ends up committing suicide with his own shears when one of his designs is rejected.

Lamentation (1930)
Martha Graham's moving, sculptural solo in which the dancer's body was encased in a tube of stretch jersey.

Do You Me? I Did (1984)
Here, as in other works of its era, Michael Clark and designers like Leigh Bowery and Bodymap said no to the traditional ballet aesthetic by donning tartan kilt and bovver boots, all-over tights with revealing holes, or a flesh-pink corset.

Nemesis (2002)
Wayne McGregor's piece for his own company Random, where dancers wearing articulated metal arm extensions resembled armoured spiders.

DANCE UNDER THE INFLUENCE OF ... PROPS

Rainforest (1968)
Merce Cunningham's dancers have to negotiate Andy Warhol's bobbing helium-filled silver pillows.

Arien (1979)
Pina Bausch's work takes place in a large pool of water inhabited, logically enough, by a hippopotamus. In other dances she's covered her stage with autumn leaves, giant Redwoods, earth and, in *Nelken*, she planted the stage with 10,000 carnations.

Bones in Pages (1993)
Saburo Teshigawara's stage is lined with 1000 books, while 1000 shoes are lined up down one side of the floor.

Rota (1996)
Deborah Colker playing with gravity. This Brazilian choreographer sets the second half of her infectious dance on a giant hamster wheel.

Songs of the Wanderers (1999)
Meditation dance theatre from Taiwanese troupe Cloud Gate, using Buddhism, Hinduism, Western modern dance – and a stage-load of dried rice.

Stage and Screen

Dancing in the dark

Sitting in the dark, in a cinema or theatre seat, is how most of us experience our dancing. At their best, these musicals imprint themselves on the collective memory. They create icons: from the elegance of Fred Astaire and Ginger Rogers to the razzle dazzle of Renée Zellweger and Catherine Zeta-Jones. From glamour to guts, from fantasy to funk, there's something here for everyone to enjoy.

If MTV and pop videos are your preferred brand of dance then be sure to check out our *Everybody Dance* chapter where you'll find a selection of the best in dance videos and even some footie.

Dance That Talks

We read each other, silently, every day via facial expressions, posture, and the pace and rhythm with which we pass through the world. It's called body language. Dance, ideally, raises such physical "speech" to the level of art.

Art with a capital "A" is all well and good, but those in musical theatre usually serve more populist ambitions. In the hands of choreographers, and specifically in the bodies they put onstage, dance is a heightened, stylised means of communication capable of whisking audiences into transports of pleasure. And whether it's the wholesome, warm-hearted exuberance of Agnes de Mille or the slinky, sexy syncopations of Bob Fosse, dance talks.

As a wordless universal language, dance can also tell stories in as simple or elaborate a fashion as necessary. Anyone who's ever seen *Swan Lake*, for instance, knows this. It doesn't matter if the teller of that particular tale is the Kirov Ballet or, in his brilliant, irreverent and much-fêted break with classical conventions, Matthew Bourne in his globetrotting production for Adventures in Motion Pictures.

Entertaining Lines

A sterling example of that stock phrase "a man of the theatre", Matthew Bourne is a balletomane who idolises Fred Astaire. He is both a life-long fan of live performance and an experienced practitioner with a wide grasp of styles and forms. The more stringent, self-absorbed abstractions of dance are alien to his creative nature. As choreographer or director, Bourne is, above all else, an entertainer. Little wonder that he refers to his work as "shows" rather than "ballets".

For him the impetus for movement is music. Using the alchemy of clear physical expression and crack timing, Bourne's dual emphasis is always on character and story. His speciality has become the non-singing "dance musical": a war-time *Cinderella*, the sexed-up melodrama of *The Car Man*, the Swinging Sixties London of *Play Without Words* (devised by Bourne's company New Adventures) and again, most famously, the gender-switching *Swan Lake*. Bourne is no slouch as a choreographic collaborator either, as his Olivier-winning work on Trevor Nunn's revival of *My Fair Lady* proved. Next, he'll be co-directing a West End version of *Mary Poppins* with Richard Eyre. His co-choreographer is Stephen Mear, who did such a galvanic job on the dances in Nunn's revival of *Anything Goes*.

Starting Lines

The quality and thrust of Bourne's work has earned him a place in a musical theatre lineage that stretches back at least to Agnes de Mille. The dances she devised for *Oklahoma!* in 1943 ushered in a new era of mature, narrative choreography on Broadway and helped kick-start the so-called Golden Age of musicals. Here song and dance stemmed from character, and were used as elements of storytelling rather than as mere diversions. The prime example is de Mille's long "dream" ballet in *Oklahoma!* when the heroine, Laurie, sorts out her confused feelings about the two men in her life, Curly and Jud. De Mille later repeated the dream device in another Rodgers and Hammerstein classic, *Carousel*. Her choreography all but eliminated the sorts of shows in which story was merely an excuse to present songs

Jerome Robbins is another key figure in the development of dance in the musical theatre. His (and composer Leonard Bernstein's) first professional job was *Fancy Free*, a one-act ballet about three sailors on shore leave in New York. Created in 1944 for Ballet Theatre, Robbins' blend of ballet and vernacular movement was an overnight sensation. It was later expanded into the Broadway hit *On the Town*, which in turn made Hollywood history as the first musical to be shot on location. Robbins achieved even greater success with *West Side Story*, a 1957 transplant of *Romeo and Juliet* to modern-day Manhattan. The musical broke new ground, not least

Liz Aggiss and Billy Cowie - *Men in the Wall* (3D image), *Capture 3*

because the substance of the show was neither spoken nor even sung words but moving bodies.

In the musical genre, battle lines are still drawn between those who favour Andrew Lloyd Webber's pop operas and fans of Stephen Sondheim's hyper-literacy. In such a context an original dance-based musical like Susan Stroman's *Contact* is rare. But the principles of musical-theatre choreography remain. Stroman, who once played the Hungarian murderess in Fosse's *Chicago*, put it succinctly: "From Fosse I learned that every step is motivated by thought. Now I only know how to do dancing that grows out of character. I stage the emotion." That is what the best show choreography manages to convey.

Doing The Business

According to the Irving Berlin standard, "there's no business like show business". For anyone who loves stage musicals, there's no theatrical high quite like the one you're sent on by a production number that pushes all the right buttons. That's certainly a vital part of the business of show dancing, which at its best can make you feel glad to be alive. Dance in stage musicals can also propel the action forward, illuminate the characters and their motivations and, basically, say things that couldn't be completely expressed in just speech or music. Below are a handful of dance-enhanced shows that, one way or another, do the business.

Oklahoma! (1943)
Agnes de Mille's joyous dances capped what she herself deemed a "remarkable and happy amalgamation of music, text, lyrics, action, scenery and costumes, which had never been approached in a light musical form before". Former Broadway gypsy Susan Stroman took on the choreography for

Most film directors carefully plot out sequences of action and even individual camera shots in advance (Alfred Hitchcock was notorious for doing this). These working drawings are known as a storyboard. This is a page from Margaret Williams' storyboard for *Outside In*, her film with CandoCo and choreographer Victoria Marks.

the 1998 National Theatre revival which later transferred to Broadway.

Carousel (1944)

Another de Mille marvel. This Rodgers and Hammerstein classic opened with a ten-minute ballet, *The Carousel Waltz*, which wordlessly set up the whole show. Kenneth MacMillan was responsible for the dances in the 1992 National Theatre revival. This was his final assignment before his fatal heart attack backstage at the Royal Opera House later that year.

Sweet Charity (1964)

Bob Fosse's upbeat adaptation of Fellini's 1957 film *The Nights of Cabiria*, about a gold-hearted and vulnerable prostitute, features such iconic numbers as *Big Spender* and *Rich Man's Frug*. Fosse himself filmed it in 1969, with Broadway-bred hoofer Shirley MacLaine stepping into Broadway icon Gwen Verdon's shoes.

A Chorus Line (1975)

Michael Bennett's unconventional and phenomenal chronicle of the trials and triumphs of a queue of legwarmer-wearing Broadway gypsies auditioning for an unseen, godlike director. The closing number, *One*, was the star of the show.

Chicago (1975)

A Chorus Line reaped the glory that year, but Bob Fosse's dazzlingly cynical period piece has, as they say in the business, got legs. The 1990s revival, supervised by top dancer-actress (and Fosse's lover) Ann Reinking, just keeps on running both in the West End and New York.

> **" "** The process of creating a music-theatre dance is not unlike cooking: you begin with your recipe and you prepare each of the ingredients individually, tasting to make sure it's to your liking, veering away from the recipe when necessary. When all the ingredients have been prepared, you add them together little by little, again tasting all the way and making adjustments. **" "**
>
> *Backstage on Broadway: Musicals and Their Makers* by Marty Bell
> (1994)

Dancin' (1978)

Fosse again, this time in an all-dance blitz pretty much unmatched until Reinking's and Verdon's posthumous tribute, *Fosse* (1999). *Dancin'* is a compilation of some of his best numbers including the ingenious *Steam Heat* routine from *The Pajama Game*. (David Bintley choreographed *The Pajama Game*, in a flawed and generally misguided West End revival of a few years ago which is best forgotten.)

Cats (1981)

British dance's great all-rounder Gillian Lynne hit a peak in this feline smash. It's the work of which she's most proud. Why? "They said that a Brit couldn't do it."

Lion King (1997)

Director-designer Julie Taymor and choreographer Garth Fagan share the kudos for this stage version of Disney's animation blockbuster. Forget the hokey aerial love ballet and revel in the animals' procession to the song *Circle of Life*. It's one of the most magical opening numbers in stage history.

Contact (2000)

Three one-acts revolving around dance, each set in a different era. The first is a sex farce spoof of Fragonard's eighteenth-century painting *Girl on a Swing*, the last is a horny, hard-edged contemporary Manhattan romance of anonymous bar pick-ups and answering machines. In the middle one, a 1950s Brooklyn mobster's abused spouse (played by ex-Royal Ballet principal Sarah Wildor in the West End) fantasises about her liberation through dance of comedic exuberance.

Kiss Me, Kate (2000)

This top-notch and superbly cast revival of Cole Porter's great musical had terrific dances by Kathleen Marshall (Rob *Chicago* Marshall's sister), including the aptly named *Too Darn Hot*.

Bombay Dreams (2002)

This glossy Bollywood-style musical is stamped with lavish, inventive dances by Scottish-born Anthony van Laast and one of Bollywood's cleverest choreographers, Farah Khan.

> **"** When I am working on something, I want to get up in the morning and look forward to going to rehearsals, work one hundred percent of myself, and come to the end exhausted and say, 'Hey, I can't wait to go back tomorrow!' That's the reason we are in the theatre, I think. **"**
>
> Graciela Daniele, former assistant to Michael Bennett and a dancer in Bob Fosse's *Chicago*, as quoted in Lawrence Thelen's *The Show Makers: Great Directors of the American Musical Theatre* (2000)

Movin' Out (2002)

Twyla Tharp raids Billy Joel's back catalogue. The result contains more dancing than has ever been seen on a Broadway stage, all at the service of a thin narrative following five friends through Vietnam-era America.

Film

Some of the greatest pleasures to be had from watching dance come from film. Think Gene Kelly soaked to the skin and high on love in *Singin' in the Rain*, or John Travolta igniting the disco craze by strutting his stuff in *Saturday Night Fever*. The gloriously over-the-top classic *The Red Shoes* was referenced (and also debunked) in the script of *A Chorus Line* as one of those movies that makes people want to become dancers. For the current generation, experts claim, *Billy Elliot* has been such an inspiration – particularly among boys. The British government is even planning to set up after-school dance centres for footloose teenagers keen for a little kinetic discipline.

Big-screen attractions, however, are not the only place where dance and film meet. At the most basic level there are performances simply recorded by the camera as a document. Alas, no film footage is known to exist of that mad marvel of early modern dance, Isadora Duncan. This was a cleverly calculated move on Duncan's part: the very absence of such documentation seals her legend.

During the latter half of the twentieth century, however, filming a performance gradually became the done thing. With the advent of video and, latterly, DVD, CD-roms and the Web, availability is no longer an issue. You can now witness great dancers in their prime, the show that you missed that created such a buzz, or some obscure piece of work from another part of the planet.

Typically, Merce Cunningham was a trailblazer in the use of video and dance. His 1981 work *Channels/Inserts* began life as a dance film that was subsequently adapted, to brilliant effect, for the stage. The award-winning *Points in Space* followed the same path – conceived for the BBC in 1986, then transferred to live performance the next year. Cunningham hasn't stopped searching and innovating either. Since about 1990 he has been using a choreographic software package called LifeForms. Devised specifically for him, it has significantly altered the ways in which his choreography is being created (on the computer, to a large degree); being danced (exceptionally tricky, because the dancers' moves are increasingly derived from what their software counterparts are capable of doing); and being perceived (more remote? more advanced? simply, and acceptably, different? and therefore, to borrow one of the words the man himself is prone to use, lively?).

Mixing It Up

With 1999's *Biped*, Cunningham strode purposefully into yet another cutting-edge crossroads of art and technology. This 45-minute marriage of actual and virtual technology utilised a computer animation process known as motion capture. Digital decor by Shelley Eshkar and Paul Kaiser lends a whole new depth of field to Cunningham's dance-making. Live dancers were sandwiched between scrims, onto which giant images – sketchy but recognisably human shapes, which can be changed in size or dimension, and into more abstract graphics – were projected.

In Twyla Tharp's 1982 dance *Bad Smells*, one of her dancers trailed about the stage with a video camera recording the brute movement like a television news reporter on war-torn location. Others, like France's Compagnie Montalvo-

Tattoo, a dance film for 92 soldiers and military band by Miranda Pennell

Hervieu, take a light-hearted tack with the possibilities of the moving image. The company is named after its artistic directors, the Spaniard José Montalvo and his French muse and associate choreographer, the ballet-trained ex-gymnast Dominique Hervieu. In all-ages entertainments like *Le Jardin Io Io Ito Ito* and its companion piece, *Paradis*, the stage becomes a combination of virtual zoo and global village, a place studded with dazzling illusions and silly sight gags. Two upstage screens host a menagerie of animals and humans who interact with live performers. In this cross-pollinated vision of paradise, circus skills meet body popping and ballet butts up against break dance. The contrasts are refreshing and the cast's fever-footed energies infectious. The meticulously-timed pre-recorded images heighten our delight.

MARGARET WILLIAMS

CHAPTER 5 • STAGE AND SCREEN

79

Pushing the Envelope

Another, similarly transporting experience of film-in-dance is Flemish choreographer Wim Vandekeybus's *Blush*, for his company Ultima Vez. Dancers leap through a slatted screen as if "into" a (projected) underwater scene, and out again. Even more startling have been the collaborations *D.A.V.E.* and *Vivisector*, between Austrian cross-media artist Klaus Obermaier and choreographer Chris Haring. Their work has been compared to *Star Trek* filtered through *The Matrix* and converted into a video game which is then rendered live. The interplay between computerised and video images and the dancers' bodies – at times fit so exactly that image and body, in effect, become one – is a case of seeing-is-believing gobsmackery.

Anjali, based in the English city of Banbury, is a company of dancers with great personality. All of its onstage members have learning disabilities. New technology was the hook of their ambitious 2003 triple-bill *WYSIWYG* (What You See Is What You Get). Luckily its subtle and varied use in each piece never superseded the company's movement, or the themes of each dance.

In Claire Russ's *Waiting Room*, the dancers occupied a curious, hermetic world of mysterious yet somehow clinical make-believe. The dancers behaved according to a secret code, sometimes mouthing words into tiny, strategically placed surveillance cameras. Only when they were all lying in a dark heap on the floor, and we were shown the just-filmed results of their performance via onstage monochromatic video monitors, was this work's carefully-plotted cleverness made apparent. Belatedly we perceived its sneaky confessional nature, with close-ups revealing phrases written on hand or shoulder ("I'm still your teddy bear" or "The camera loves me"). The net effect was funny and unsettling.

Camera Ready

Another major area of the dance/film crossover is movement conceived – choreographed, really – expressly for the camera. This splits into several strands: bigger-budgeted, feature-length films, the lucrative music video and, last but by no means least, the huge and thriving independent or, for want of a better word, screen dance scene. The latter encompasses work in which dance and film are married and of equal importance; where the collision of moving image and choreography creates a product that can only exist on screen; and where the collaboration between a director and a choreographer may be so closely intertwined that the notion of separate defined roles is a fiction. This includes dance films broadcast on television and/or presented in cinemas, often in festivals.

It's worth noting that, even if a small, independent dance film is being screened at some ungodly hour, the potential audience is still enormous. But when the BBC film *Cross Channel* (made by choreographer Lea Anderson and filmmaker Margaret Williams and currently compulsory viewing

LITZA BIXLER
COMMERCIAL SUCCESS

Born in Denver, Colorado, where she trained as a performer, director and photographer, Litza Bixler later completed a Master's degree in choreography in the UK. She moved to London in the 1990s but continues to work around the world. Her award-winning commercial and promotional work includes *LEVIS Twisted*, and videos with music artists from Basement Jaxx and Natalie Imbruglia to Sophie Ellis Bextor and Ronan Keating.

As high-profile as these credits may sound, the reality can leave something to be desired. "When you're hired as a choreographer in film or video," Bixler says, "a lot has to be let go of. It's the polar opposite of ballet and contemporary dance. If it's a commercial you're working on, it can be soul-destroying; it's all about making the product look good, not about the dancing being right. With music videos it's about selling the artist and making them look good, rather than doing something innovative for the sake of exploring the medium.

"As a dancer I never got to the point of professional expertise," Bixler confesses. But there are advantages to linking reasonable physical proficiency with a magpie-like sensibility. "As long as I'm interested I'll learn a new technique to a moderate point of mastery and then move on. Your vocabulary gets bigger and bigger, and you begin to recognise your own strengths. And whereas being a jack of all trades worked against me in other art forms, in film it's all paid off."

As an up-and-coming director her short films include *Heart Thief* for Channel 4, and she occasionally makes work for the stage, such as a 2004 solo for Lorena Randi, a principal dancer with Michael Clark. She's now itching to choreograph a bona fide musical film, either her own or somebody else's. "On a musical the director and the choreographer should be one and the same person," Bixler believes. "But even with a 'pure' narrative, a background in dance is very useful because of what you know about rhythm, timing and space. I've gradually learned the medium's weaknesses. The camera can be distracting. Don't get so excited when shooting a film that it takes precedence over content. Don't overuse close-ups, let a scene breathe.

"You also have to understand whether the camera's moving or not and how that will affect the dynamic of the choreography. It's almost like working with a puzzle, envisaging in your head how something is going to be cut together to make something seamless."

Bixler has landed gigs on several feature-length films: the zombie comedy *Shaun of the Dead*, a remake of *Alfie* starring Jude Law and a whimsical period comedy with Sam Rockwell called *Piccadilly Jim*. "One of the Steadicam shots I did in *Shaun* was all done to counts, choreographed for the camera like a musical dance sequence. Light cue, count two; camera tracking, count five; music cue… That gave it a more secure and predictable outcome."

Bixler's advice for budding Bob Fosses? "You can go to film school, but the best way to learn is by being on the set and watching other directors work.

"Yes, it's about being creative, but also about knowing how to get the best out of people and deal with your own feelings. You have to be able to handle stress. When the relationship is not working, directors feel like their toes are being trod upon. In that kind of situation choreographers must eat humble pie."

for GCSE S-level studies in dance) was broadcast in prime time just after *Mad Max 2*, it got the best part of two million viewers and a plethora of positive calls to the BEEB switchboard along the lines of "I don't know what it is, but I like it". A dance-maker would have to sell out a 300-seat venue every night for fifteen years to achieve the same number of spectators as that single TV screening.

Britain's *Dance for Camera* series, which ran from 1991 to 2003, was key in the development of screen dance. More than fifty short films were commissioned in total, including bona fide masterpieces like *Outside In*, by Margaret Williams and Victoria Marks with CandoCo Dance Company, and *Boy*, by Peter Anderson and Rosemary Lee. The potential of screen dance continues to broaden. Recent projects such as *Capture* have pushed the boundaries of what type of screen dance can exist, thanks to such works as the interactive dance CD-rom *Waterfall* by Richard Lord.

Captured

Assembled in 2004, *Capture 3* was a touring collection of screen-based installations, more conventional single-screen films and new media works commissioned and funded, for a third consecutive year, by the Arts Council England. The two installations were wonderful and memorable experiences. You needed to don 3-D glasses to enhance the seminal four-screen, stereoscopic installation *Men in the Wall* by the Brighton-based team of Liz Aggiss and Billy Cowie. Situated against various backdrops (day, night, urban, coastal, etc), each male – a mixed batch of builds, temperaments and nationalities – dwells in his own walled square. They talk, sing, play music and move in a fashion stamped with the Aggiss/Cowie signature of quirky-humoured poetry and skewed beauty.

Nic Sandiland's and Rosemary Lee's *Remote Dancing* was an enticing series of short solos – interactive pas de deux, really – which occur in up to four separate corridors. Single viewers traversed each long space towards screens occupied, one at a time, by dancers whose ages spanned the generations. The viewer's own movement triggered, advanced and rewound both the film image (set initially in a black void, then outdoors) and the sound (by Graeme Miller). The longer you spent with your screen counterparts, the more you wanted to move in response to – and thereby influence – their motion and rhythms. Great fun.

Celluloid Hoofers
Great dance film moments

In some respects, the feature film industry is all about dance. Choreographer and director Bob Fosse knew that. "We're dealing with moving pictures," he once remarked. "If you're not moving the camera, then you must be moving something through that frame, because moving pictures are what movies are all about."

In the silent era there were prodigious clowns like Charlie Chaplin and Buster Keaton, whose ingenious acrobatics and expressive use of the body are indelibly imprinted on cultural consciousness. The advent of sound ushered in the lavish song and dance numbers, which for a good three decades yielded some of the most heavenly sights – the embarrassment of riches that Fred Astaire gave us, say, or Gene Kelly at the Metro-Goldwyn-Mayer dream factory.

Even earlier Busby Berkeley was wielding the camera with supreme, kaleidoscopic illogic through some of the best musicals of the 1930s (*42nd Street*, *Footlight Parade*, *Gold Diggers of 1933* and *Gold Diggers of 1935*). In her book *America Dances* (1980), Agnes de Mille remembered a dreamy chunk from one such extravagant production number as "a chorus of thirty-two girls at grand pianos, which swung and fanned into view on slowly unfolding platforms, like the petals of a flower".

Within three decades the big studios began dying off or reforming, as a string of expensive flops starring Julie Andrews and Barbra Streisand effectively killed off the big-screen musical. Even so, European directors who love the movies – Jean-Luc Godard and, later, Pedro Almodóvar, for example – have often paid homage to American musicals in their own work. There was a modicum of rebirth for the genre, and for dance on the big screen in general, thanks to the success of pictures like *Dirty Dancing*, *Fame*, *Flashdance* and

Grease, most of which contained some dance performance milieu or motive. But however fondly one may feel about these and other pictures, they just ain't got the transcendental class of the great movie musicals. Maybe *Moulin Rouge* and *Chicago* will kick-start a renaissance, but don't hold your breath. But do get the *Moulin Rouge* DVD. One of its special features is all of the uncut dance sequences. And let's not forget that Bollywood is still thriving. If you're in need of an extravaganza fix this is the place to find it.

In the meantime, below is a pretty wild bunch of either dance-slanted films or those which contain some noteworthy movement material – from animation to martial arts. Such is the pervasive power of the cinema that even the most casual movie-goer could probably come up with a raft of additions.

The Four Horsemen of the Apocalypse (1921)

Silent heart-throb Rudolph Valentino assured himself a place in movie history by dancing the tango in this World War I drama.

Our Dancing Daughters (1928)

Joan Crawford helped unleash – and capitalise upon – a dance craze by letting rip with the Charleston in this tail-end-of-the-silent-era romantic drama. The picture, and her avid

> **"** One of the best things about screen dance is that it's still open territory. Anyone's allowed to go out there and explore, and everyone's going to explore in different ways, so it has the richness of being this area where you can still try all kinds of things. **"**
>
> David Hinton, director

dancing, helped turn this ferociously determined jazz baby into a major star.

Fantasia (1940)

Ostriches in pointe shoes and hippos in tutus in Disney's proto-psychedelic feature-length musical cartoon.

The Gang's All Here (1943)

The Lady in the Tutti Frutti Hat features that peerless embodiment of high-voltage South American camp, Carmen Miranda, plus a platoon of chorines manipulating giant bananas. Who else but Busby Berkeley (now in blazing colour) could've cooked up this eye-popping epitome of extravagance?

The Three Caballeros (1944)

Disney doing its delirious bit for Latin American relations in an animated feature with live-action bits. Loaded with goodies: multiple floral Donald Ducks doing pirouettes; dancing cacti; disembodied kisses; and spun-sugar surrealism as Donald dances on galaxies of stars.

Summer Stock (1950)

One of Judy Garland's off-screen problem pictures. Which ones weren't? It contains her rousingly sung and danced rendition of *Get Happy*, backed by a snappy male chorus.

> **"** The camera doesn't have energy, it doesn't have volume and it doesn't have three-dimensional qualities. **"**
>
> Choreographer Siobhan Davies sides with the nay-sayers

Garland looks terrific in a short black jacket and over-one-eye hat. A career highlight.

The 5,000 Fingers of Dr T (1953)

Eugene Loring – who choreographed the popular cowboy ballet *Billy the Kid* and was Fred Astaire's collaborator on the 1957 *Funny Face* – staged the testosterone-charged underground ballet in this utterly off-beat children's nightmare musical.

Gentlemen Prefer Blondes (1953)

Fosse precursor Jack Cole helps turn Marilyn Monroe into box-office gold. The tone is set from the stride-and-bump opening with statuesque mate Jane Russell, *Two Little Girls From Little Rock*, and reaches a peak with MM cooing *Diamonds Are a Girl's Best Friend*. This is another source of cultural cupboard-raiding by Material Girl Madonna.

Kiss Me, Kate (1953)

Made in 3-D, with Ann Miller tapping away like a manic drummer. Choreographed by Hermes Pan, but Bob Fosse staged his own bit, a short duet that would serve as an early blueprint for his Broadway style.

Seven Brides for Seven Brothers (1954)

An MGM heart-warmer. Michael Kidd's central barn-raising dance is plain magnificent.

West Side Story (1961)

Agnes de Mille wrote that herein Jerome Robbins achieved the cinematic/choreographic equivalent of "breaking the sound barrier".

Bye Bye Birdie (1963)

One of the high spots of this big, splashy Broadway adaptation is *A Lot of Livin' to Do*, a jivey nightclub number choreographed with memorable quirkiness by Onna White and lovingly shot by director George Sidney. The camera practically drools over his sizzling, shapely star, Ann-Margret.

A Clockwork Orange (1971)

Remember Malcolm McDowell's vicious mockery of *Singin' in the Rain*?

Cabaret (1972)

Could this be the best movie version ever of a Broadway musical? It's Fosse's genius that here – and in *Lenny* (not a musical) or *All That Jazz* – practically everything is choreographed for the camera.

The Turning Point (1977)

A sentimental favourite, and probably one of the best narratives set in a ballet milieu since *The Red Shoes*. Plus, Mikhail Baryshnikov in his movie debut.

Raging Bull (1980)

As film-maker David Hinton says about Martin Scorsese's masterpiece in Sherril Dodds' *Dance on Screen* (2001), "the boxing sequences are fantastically powerful movement sequences".

Big (1988)

Who could forget boy-in-a-man's-body Tom Hanks and his boss dancing on the toy store's giant xylophone?

Strictly Ballroom (1992)

Milieu exuberant kitsch, Baz Luhrmann's breakthrough first film and a landmark in Australian cinema. A ballroom-dancing champion performs his own steps in an important championship, teaming up with a novice in a bid for artistic freedom on the dancefloor.

Pulp Fiction (1994)

Uma Thurman and sock-wearing comeback king John Travolta get in the coolest groove in Quentin Tarantino's modern classic.

Everyone Says I Love You (1996)

Woody Allen and an airborne Goldie Hawn on the banks of the Seine. Isn't it romantic?

The Full Monty (1997)

A global favourite moment: the guys in the bank queue.

Matrix (1999)
Crouching Tiger, Hidden Dragon (2000)

Two in one from fight and movement master Yuen Wo-Ping. Would you choose the latter's combative dance in the treetops or the former's speed-warped rooftop and underground battles?

Talk to Her (2001)

Any film that starts out with two grown men crying in their seats while watching a Pina Bausch dance deserves affection and respect. Thank you, Pedro Almodóvar. A nice turn from Geraldine Chaplin, too, as a venerable ballet bird.

Dracula: Pages from Virgin's Diary (2002)

Guy Maddin's stunningly stylised ballet adaptation of Bram Stoker's bloodsucking shocker features members of the Royal Winnipeg Ballet.

Kill Bill Volume 1 (2003)

Thurman and Tarantino are at it again. Yuen Wo-Ping, too. Here Uma's a figure of concentrated mayhem and kick-ass empowerment.

The Company (2003)

Robert Altman does dance with the help of Chicago's Joffrey Ballet; co-producer, co-author and star Neve Campbell; and some pretty hideous choreography. Malcolm McDowell pops up again, this time as the benevolent despot of a company director: "It's not the steps, babies, it's what's inside that counts!"

Zatoichi (2004)

Director and star Takehisa Kitano hiked up the gory effects in this rollicking samurai slaughter-fest "so the viewer can concentrate on the choreographic element of sword fighting". Note the percussive field dance in rain and mud and the sensationally celebratory tap finale – "flamboyant and funky" as *Time Out* so rightly put it.

Movers and Shakers

A dance world Who's Who

The planet is crawling with choreographers – gifted and great, no-talent or wanna-be. We can't possibly list them all here, nor even attempt to cite the best and brightest (or merely best-publicised) in every country.

Nevertheless, here are some subjectively selected names to watch out for. Inevitably some notable people, and whole swathes of thriving dance culture, will have been left out. Apologies in advance for any sins of omission.

Best of British

Richard Alston

Renowned for a choreographic style based on elegantly crafted musicality, Alston was one of the first students at the then-new London Contemporary Dance School (1967). He performed on the very first night of the first Dance Umbrella. After working with the now-defunct London Contemporary Dance Theatre, he became director of Rambert Dance Company (1986–93). Alston is now artistic director at The Place, where his own company is based.

Lea Anderson

The lynchpin of the (female) Cholmondeleys and (male) Featherstonehaughs, a unique forum for an intricate, gestural style threading off-beat humour through its keenly observed fabric. The two sides of Anderson's choreographic coin united for a twentieth birthday tour in 2004.

Laurie Booth

Best known as an intense improvisational soloist who incorporates martial arts, contemporary styles and a body training system called gyrotonic expansion. Booth trained in physical theatre but found his work appealing to dance audiences. His early political themes have given way to a more spiritual realm.

Matthew Bourne

From indie beginnings with Adventures in Motion Pictures, Bourne is now the commercial megastar of British contemporary dance. Best known for his male take on *Swan Lake*, Bourne's sly humour and instinctive musicality are to the fore in his 1960s pastiche *Play without Words*. He co-directs and choreographs the upcoming West End production of *Mary Poppins*.

Kim Brandstrup

A classical stylist working in the contemporary idiom, Copenhagen-born Brandstrup has kept true faith with the art of storytelling through dance with his Arc Dance Company. Shakespeare and Dostoyevsky have been among his sources.

Carol Brown

The work of this brainy dance artist encompasses installation, architecture and new technologies. You can't always warm to it, but Brown is an innovator and explorer who doesn't want to lose sight of the human body amidst all the perceptual "tricks" she conjures round it.

The Laban Centre

Jonathan Burrows

Turning his Royal Ballet heritage on its head, Burrows pares down choreography to lean, clean essentials. His famously simple, eloquent dance *Hands* – starring guess what – has been filmed. In recent years Burrows has been pushing boundaries via subtle, anti-spectacular collaborations with theatre director Jan Ritsema (*Weak Dance Strong Questions*) and composer Matteo Fargion (*Both Sitting Duet*).

Rosemary Butcher

Doyenne of independent dance. A radical who combines plenty of non-dance influences with an intellectual and conceptual approach. Unafraid to go where no other choreographer has been before, Butcher's recent piece, *WHITE*, was based on Captain Scott's ill-fated expedition to the Antarctic. Throughout her career she has favoured unconventional performance spaces.

Nigel Charnock

From his roots as DV8 co-founder, Renaissance man Charnock has gone on to star as dancer, comedian, writer, actor and singer in a range of solo and group projects. Currently directing the Helsinki National Dance Theatre – Finland's gain is Britain's loss.

Michael Clark

The former Royal Ballet wunderkind shot to fame with his punk-pop Leigh Bowery–clad company in the 1980s. His spiky, deceptively chaotic deconstruction of classical ballet still has considerable mileage left in it on the evidence of recent work like *O My Goddess*.

Siobhan Davies

Influential on the British dance scene since the 1970s, Davies has won a devoted audience with her often austere, clear-eyed yet mercurial dance stylings. Recent moves towards site-specific work and collaborations – eg, playwright Caryl Churchill on *Plants and Ghosts* – find her still pushing in new directions.

Yael Flexer

Her company Bedlam is frequently humorous, sometimes tender, and full of the quirks of an all-too-recognisable humanity. There's an honesty about the ideas and the performances that is very appealing.

Javier De Frutos

A bravura solo artist of no little cheek (a bare-buttocked *Rite of Spring* figures on his CV), this Venezuelan-born choreographer is in demand in Britain and abroad. His brand of decadent glamour has breathed extra life into the likes of Rambert and Can*do*Co.

Wendy Houstoun

Another graduate of the class of DV8, Houstoun has forged a fine solo career built around her considerable talents as comedienne, dancer and social observer. A wit so sharp she could cut herself.

Shobana Jeyasingh

Into fusion before it was fashionable, Jeyasingh has been a key figure in the cross-pollination of Eastern and Western dance styles. Elements of classical Indian bharata natyam combine with a distinctly Anglo-Indian sensibility.

Akram Khan

Taking the best from his mix of North Indian classical dance style, kathak, and contemporary dance training, Khan has swept to the top of the British dance tree thanks to his mesmeric performance presence and an intense choreographic style high on passion and atmosphere.

Charles Linehan

The quiet man of British dance. A choreographer who works intently and intensely to create whispered conversations overheard from the next room. If you pay close attention to what he's up to you will be rewarded with an exceptional experience that will intrigue you for days to come.

Russell Maliphant

A physically stunning performer with a style that blends balletic grace, gymnastic muscle and capoeira agility, Maliphant now has a small company of dancers able to tackle his demanding moves.

Wayne McGregor

He founded the forward-looking Random Dance in 1992 but has also choreographed for numerous others including Rambert and the Royal Ballet. McGregor reinvents the human body, and his interest in science and technology led him to make *Nemesis*, a piece where dancers wore insect-like prosthetics to extend their limbs.

Lloyd Newson

Co-founder and mainspring of DV8, Britain's most influential physical theatre company of the past two decades. Sexual politics and emotional muscle combine in a compelling mix of movement and drama. Key works include *Dead Dreams of Monochrome Men*, *Strange Fish* and *Enter Achilles*, all available on video.

Henri Oguike

A founder member of the Richard Alston Dance Company, Oguike launched his own company in 1999. His work has a sophisticated clarity and energy and a vibrant relationship with music.

Luca Silvestrini and Bettina Strickler

Take one Italian and one Swiss and what do you get? Protein Dance, the funniest English company currently doing the rounds. Talking of rounds, the duo's high-voltage reality dance *Publife* is performed in real pubs rather than in the theatre.

Yolande Snaith

A mistress of the cunningly constructed prop and costume, Snaith's quintessentially British take on physical theatre is a timeless feast for the eyes and mind.

Jasmin Vardimon

Favouring a theatrical slant on dance, Vardimon's physically charged choreography is laced with dark humour and carries the tang of personal experience – as seen in the recent *Lullaby*, a starkly humorous reflection on hospital horrors.

Fin Walker

Her distinctive movement is full of innovation, drive and stop-start motion. Walker works in such close collaboration with contemporary composer Ben Park that they've dubbed their company Walker Dance Park Music.

Continental Darlings

Pina Bausch

Based in Germany, in demand around the globe. The single most significant ideas guru of the past three decades. Without her kaleidoscopic take on dance theatre, which she virtually invented, dance today would look very different.

Jerome Bel

One of the key French conceptualists. Bel's questioning, dry-humoured work ranges from *Shirtology*, in which a lone dancer keeps doffing slogan- and image-bearing T-shirts, and the vastly enjoyable ensemble extravaganza *The Show Must Go On*, an ironic paean to the potency of popular music.

Boris Charmatz

Whether his work charms the pants off you or merely deeply annoys, there's no denying the versatility and reach of this

Maresa von Stockert & Tilted Co: *Beyond the Seven Seas*

Frenchman. No two dances are alike. One, featuring three bottom-baring dancers, was set in a specially constructed backstage tower. In another, one spectator at a time lay atop a cushy faux piano and watched weirdo dance videos as the lighting and sound kept altering as if of their own accord.

Sidi Larbi Cherkaoui

A star attraction in Alain Platel's Les Ballets C de la B, this slightly built Flemish-Moroccan choreographer dances like a slippery angel. His own notably non-ageist, "multi-culti" works *Rien de Rien* and *Foi* have garnered acclaim for their ambition, humanity, and epic yet quirky sense of theatre.

Mats Ek

The son of Birgit Cullberg, founder of Sweden's Cullberg Ballet, Ek combines earthy body language with a gutsy streak of surrealism. He is best known for his wickedly inventive retellings of the classics – a hugely sympathetic "village idiot" *Giselle* who winds up in an asylum, or a drug addict *Sleeping Beauty*.

Frédéric Flamand

The artistic director of the Belgian company Charleroi Danses/Plan K is a shining example of someone who wants to mix and match art forms and collaborate on ideas, especially with architects such as Zaha Hadid.

William Forsythe

American born, Frankfurt based. Top player. Began by deconstructing his ballet traditions with fierce, fast dances on pointe. He's now virtually abandoned this route in favour of further explorations.

Emio Greco | PC

Working with his partner, director Pieter CC. Scholten, Greco is forging an original, agitated and exacting movement language that appeals equally to body and brain. He's an exciting soloist. The pair's stagecraft, especially in terms of lighting and space, is impeccable.

Gilles Jobin

Swiss-born dance-maker, based in London but thus far achieving greater acceptance abroad. His dances pulse with ideas, but always rooted in the body. Jobin made his mark with a series of dances that exposed naked flesh in the intimate glare of high-intensity light.

Anne Teresa De Keersmaeker

This hugely significant Belgian choreographer made her name with minimalist abstractions like the mesmerising duet *Fase*, for her initially all-female company Rosas. Yet she also favours elaborate, theatrically expressive productions that feature text. Her influence was secured by the formation of the Brussels-based school PARTS.

Jiří Kylián

Revered on the Continent, less loved in America, Kylián's Nederlands Dans Theater has created a house style that has permeated the up-market end of the contemporary scene since the late 1970s. His early works were virtually modern ballet without the pointe shoes. Now they're a crotchety mix of often-elaborate props and angular bodies.

Maguy Marin

One of France's leading lights, Marin has never stopped

testing the artistic waters with her loyal company. Works include a magical doll-house *Cinderella*, a housing-estate *Coppélia* and the bleak but beautiful, Beckett-inspired "comedy" *May B*, in which a chalky-faced cast slump and shuffle about in padded costumes.

Ohad Naharin

Israel's leading choreographer creates strong dance-theatre marked by vigorous ensemble movement and bold design. His works for Batsheva Dance Company can be severe and way-out, and yet his *Minus 16* is a crowd-pulling favourite and one of the best audience-participation dances ever.

Angelin Preljocaj

This French choreographer has paid fresh, unconventional homage to Ballets Russes classics such as *Les Noces* and *The Rite of Spring*. He's also staged works for the Paris Opera Ballet and New York City Ballet, but it is with his own company in Aix that he probes for new ways of moving the body which can be simultaneously radical and beautiful. His futurist version of *Romeo and Juliet* is set in a totalitarian state.

La Ribot

She's been compared to Salvador Dalí crossed with Lucille Ball. This British-based Spanish redhead likes to get her kit off, using her own body as both canvas and installation in an ongoing, for-sale series of original dance performances entitled *Distinguished Pieces*. Wacky and wonderful.

Saburo Teshigawara

This cultish Japanese choreographer mounts disturbing, poetic and ambiguous productions for his company KARAS, in which he himself, a superb dancer, occasionally performs. Even his solos are conceived on a large, yet still human scale. Lately he's been working brilliantly with blind or partially-sighted dancers.

Wim Vandekeybus

This former wunderkind burst on the scene in the late 1980s with a prop-heavy brand of physical riskiness that came to be known as Euro-crash – that is, dancers trying to avoid smashing into each other or, conversely, doing just that. He's still pushing this dynamic envelope via shows like *In Spite of Wishing and Wanting* and *Blush*, for his Brussels-based company Ultima Vez.

Greats of the States

Alvin Ailey (1931–1989)

A Graham-trained dancer who formed his own company Alvin Ailey American Dance Theatre in 1958. One of the most prominent black dancers of his generation, Ailey drew on the African-American experience in his choreography, combining jazz, classical, contemporary and black dance styles.

Trisha Brown

One of the founders of the Judson Dance Theatre in the 1960s, a breeding ground for post-modern choreographers. Her stripped-down, minimal works were based on everyday movement and rebelling against theatrical dance traditions. She has softened a bit in her older age, allowing music, backdrops and costumes to creep in.

Merce Cunningham

The godfather of contemporary dance, Cunningham is still

creating work in his eighties. He danced with Martha Graham in the early 1940s before leaving to make his own work, full of busy, graceful, abstract movement and avant-garde ideas. He famously collaborated with composer John Cage and more recently created pieces with music by Radiohead and Sigur Ros.

Garth Fagan

Known to the world as the choreographer for the stage version of *The Lion King*, the Jamaican-born Fagan has run his own eclectic contemporary company since the beginning of the 1970s.

Martha Graham (1894–1991)

She only started dancing at the age of 22 but went on to revolutionise the dance world. Graham's weighty, expressive, dramatic style was based on her own body and forceful personality. Graham died in 1991 but, despite some financial troubles and lengthy legal battles, her company has survived and returned to the stage in 2003.

Bill T. Jones

A charismatic dancer and choreographer, Jones formed Bill T. Jones/Arnie Zane Dance Company with his partner, who died of AIDS in 1988. Jones's work combines numerous dance and theatre influences with politics and autobiography, covering themes such as homosexuality and racism.

Mark Morris

In his teens Morris danced with a Balkan folk troupe and studied flamenco as well as ballet. All these ingredients influence his eclectic approach to movement. He often uses undancerly figures (Morris himself is quite rotund these days) but the work is always very watchable, and very musical. His evening-length piece set to Handel's *L'Allegro, il penseroso ed il moderato* (1988) was a huge hit and remains a major work in modern dance.

Stephen Petronio

A pacey, energetic and athletic style defines Petronio's work along with a long list of hip collaborators in the fields of fashion, music and art. Petronio never shies away from controversy, once making a work which essentially consisted of he and his then-lover Michael Clark cavorting in bed together.

Paul Taylor

A former swimmer who went on to dance with Martha Graham's company before setting up his own, Taylor is one of the greats of modern American dance. His signature style is joyful, humorous and spirited, although the choreographer has been known to show his darker side. His works are danced by both modern and ballet companies around the world.

Twyla Tharp

From rigorous intellectual experimentation in the 1960s to the queen of Broadway forty years later, this American choreographer has covered all the bases in dance. She began eschewing music and any hint of virtuosity in her modern dance language, but evolved into one of the most successful ballet choreographers, responsible for marrying the high art of the classical technique with the influences of American popular culture, especially its music. She ran her own company for thirty years, enjoyed a long relationship with American Ballet Theatre, choreographed several Hollywood films and created the immensely successful Broadway musical, *Movin' Out*, in 2002.

Big in Ballet

Frederick Ashton (1904–1988)

Elegant, lyrical and often witty, he was the main architect behind the "English" style with its sparkling footwork, fluidity and novel twists of the body. He revered the academic style embodied in the ballets of Marius Petipa. In a creative career of almost 60 years his output ranged far and wide, from the comedy of *La Fille mal gardée* to pure-dance pieces such as *Symphonic Variations* and *Rhapsody*.

George Balanchine (1904–1983)

The big daddy of American ballet was born in St Petersburg, escaped to the West when he hooked up with Diaghilev's Les Ballets Russes: *Apollo* (1928) was his first major work and also the world's first neo-classical ballet, giving a modern jazzy thrust to traditional technique. He was lured to America in 1934, set up a ballet school, later founding New York City Ballet for which he created around 400 works. At the heart of every one of them is the belief that dance is music made visible.

David Bintley

Artistic director of Birmingham Royal Ballet since 1995, he is now best known for his full-evening ballets (ten of them to date) based on British history, *Edward II*, literature *Far from the Madding Crowd*, *Hobson's Choice*, and legend *Arthur*. Bintley has also created several fine plotless one-act works such as *Tombeaux*, *Flowers of the Forest* and *Allegri Diversi*.

August Bournonville (1805–1879)

Nineteenth-century Danish choreographer whose ballets, such as *La Sylphide*, define Romantic ballet. Key features of his choreography are an airy bounce and fleet footwork which was particularly brilliant in solos for the men. As a result, an unusual number of the world's great male dancers have been from the Royal Danish Ballet, including Peter Martins, who now directs New York City Ballet, and the current Royal Ballet star Johan Kobborg.

Mikhail (Michel) Fokine (1880–1942)

Early twentieth-century pioneer, best known today for *Chopiniana* (later called *Les Sylphides*), *The Firebird* and *Petrushka*. As a choreographer at St Petersburg's Maryinsky Theatre, he felt hamstrung by tradition and left to join Diaghilev's Ballets Russes in Paris. He believed that dance, music and design should share equal status, and rejected the idea that a blanket style could be applied to any subject.

Kenneth MacMillan (1929–1992)

British ballet moderniser and one-time Royal Ballet director, MacMillan reinvented the story-ballet as psychological drama tackling such subjects as madness, lust and guilt. His *Romeo and Juliet* and *Manon* are popular repertory staples around the world. But it's his shorter pieces such as *Gloria*, *Song of the Earth* and *The Judas Tree* that contain his best inspiration, with taut, expressionist movement motifs conveying a gamut of conflicted feeling.

Vaslav Nijinsky (1889–1950)

A key figure of twentieth-century modernism. As a star dancer of Diaghilev's Ballets Russes his exotic stage persona and amazing skills drove audiences wild. His radical choreographic exploits broke every rule in the book: *L'Après-midi d'un faune* (overtly erotic), *Jeux* (same-sex flirtation) and *Le Sacre du printemps* (savagely animalistic). His succès de scandale was short-lived. At the age of 27 he began showing signs of instability, and spent most of the rest of his life in mental hospitals.

Marius Petipa (1818–1910)

The Sleeping Beauty and *Swan Lake*, twin peaks of nineteenth-century classical dance, are just two of the many works by Petipa, the single most influential choreographer in the history of ballet. A Frenchman who spent most of his life in St Petersburg, he forged a style marrying the refinement of the French and Italian schools with the grandeur of Tsarist Russia. *The Nutcracker* was also his baby, though ill health forced him to delegate the step-making to his assistant, Lev Ivanov, who had also collaborated with him on *Swan Lake*.

Jerome Robbins (1918–1998)

The all-American Robbins straddled the divide between highbrow and low. His first major choreographic work was the phenomenally successful *Fancy Free*, a story about three sailors on shore leave which he later adapted into the Broadway musical *On the Town*. He also choreographed *West Side Story*, *Gypsy* and *Fiddler on the Roof*, and more than fifty one-act works for New York City Ballet, including *The Concert* – a comic masterpiece.

Antony Tudor (1909–1987)

Tudor was the British ballet catch that got away. Discovered by Marie Rambert, he joined her company in 1930 at the age of 21. Two of his most enduring ballets, *Lilac Garden* and *Dark Elegies*, come from this time. Both explored new psychological avenues in dance. In 1939 Tudor moved to New York where he stayed, working mainly with American Ballet Theatre. Though far from prolific, he was a sharp observer of human behaviour, and was among the first choreographers to focus on the interior lives of ordinary men and women.

Christopher Wheeldon

Throughout the 1990s the cry of "where next for ballet?" grew increasingly desperate. The deaths of Ashton and MacMillan in Britain, and Balanchine and Robbins in America left a gaping hole waiting to be filled by a choreographer who would respect ballet's stylistic traditions, but also carry it forward into new territories. Wheeldon started making pieces as a young dancer at the Royal Ballet, but his career took off when he was taken up by New York City Ballet where he is now resident choreographer. One of his latest commissions, *Mesmerics*, has been a hit for George Piper Dances.

UK Repertory Companies

CandoCo

Some leading choreographers have created works for this company which features a mix of dancers both with and without physical disabilities. Among those helping to prove that this company needs to be neither patronised nor ghettoised have been Javier De Frutos, Siobhan Davies and Stephen Petronio, plus the duo of Luca Silvestrini and Bettina Strickler.

Ⓦ www.candoco.co.uk

Diversions

The national dance company of Wales tours widely on its home turf with an ambitious mix of work by native dance-makers like Sean Tuan John (he of the kitsch-pop sensibility) and foreign guests like Finland's masterful Tommi Kitti and Spain's Toni Mira.

Ⓦ www.diversionsdance.co.uk

George Piper Dances

Michael Nunn and William Trevitt created the *Ballet Boyz* dance documentaries for Channel 4. Their sharp, successful and enterprising company (George and Piper are their middle names) has as its raison d'être the notion of commissioning new choreography. Their energy and enterprise are the reasons why you're reading this book.

Ⓦ www.gpdances.com

Phoenix Dance Theatre

Darshan Singh Bhuller now heads this Leeds-based troupe, which has gone through many tribulations and transformations since it was founded in 1980 by five black men. Bhuller's ensemble has an attractive versatility showcased in dances by the likes of Fin Walker, Henri Oguike, Maresa von Stockert and Bhuller himself.

Ⓦ www.phoenixdancetheatre.co.uk

Rambert Dance Company

Britain's longest established dance troupe began life as a ballet company in 1926, switched to a modern repertory in 1966. Mark Baldwin is the current director. Company dancer Rafael Bonachela, who has already created seven dances for

Rambert since 1999, is now its associate resident choreographer. Continuing to forge strong links with contemporary composers and dance-makers, Baldwin is building on the company's wide-ranging repertoire (including works from former director Christopher Bruce, whose legacy and influence on dance extends well beyond the UK), as well as Merce Cunningham, Wayne McGregor, Javier De Frutos, Fin Walker and, in the pipeline for late 2004, Michael Clark.

Ⓦ www.rambert.org.uk

Ricochet Productions

Founded by Kate Gowar and Karin Fisher-Potisk, this dancer-led company has commissioned new work by top contemporary choreographers like Stephen Petronio, Javier De Frutos and Russell Maliphant. They're not timid about new artistic avenues: witness their 2004 rebirth as a production outfit free to try its hand at dance-based films or installations.

Ⓦ ricochetdance.com

Scottish Dance Theatre

Scotland's flagship contemporary troupe. Janet Smith's immensely likeable dancers are loaded with personality, but never at the expense of skill. She commissions new work from companies (New Art Club) or individuals (Jan de Schynkel), besides being a choreographer in her own right.

Ⓦ www.scottishdancetheatre.com

UK Ballet Companies

Birmingham Royal Ballet

Originally an offshoot of the Royal Ballet, choreographer

David Bintley's now-autonomous BRB proves that you don't have to be in the capital to make your mark in the dance world.

ⓦ www.brb.org.uk

English National Ballet

Under former dancer Matz Skoog's direction, "The People's Ballet Company" tours widely with a blend of classics and freshly commissioned work. Super-celebrity Victoria Beckham is a fan.

ⓦ www.ballet.org.uk

Northern Ballet Theatre

Led by choreographer David Nixon, this popular Leeds-based troupe unites dance and drama in original productions such as *Wuthering Heights*, *Dracula* and *A Midsummer Night's Dream*.

ⓦ www.northernballettheatre.co.uk

The Royal Ballet

Some of the world's best dancers perform classic and new choreography from their grand home at the Royal Opera House in Covent Garden.

ⓦ www.royalballet.org

Scottish Ballet

Artistic director and choreographer (and ex-Royal Ballet principal) Ashley Page is bringing new, cutting-edge lustre to this Glasgow-based troupe.

ⓦ www.scottishballet.org

A Very Rough Guide to Ballet Plots

Dance may be an international language, but that doesn't mean you can always tell what's going on. This is true even of the warhorses which are the staples of the classical repertoire, hence the two- or three-page synopsis you'll find in most ballet programmes. But what happens if the lights go down before you have time to read it? The following thumbnail descriptions offer a brief – and none too serious – idea of what to expect. That ballet can and does rise so far above the ludicrousness of its plots remains one of the marvels of the art form.

La Bayadère

A sultry tale of sex, drugs and contract killing set in Imperial Russia's idea of India, where a noble warrior might get stoned on the day of his wedding and the bride dispose of her rival by means of a deadly snake bite. Neither of them, however, has reckoned on the lure of love beyond the grave, or the hallucinatory powers of hashish to summon up 32 girls in white tutus.

Coppélia

Set in a Tyrolean village where all the girls wear identical pinnies. Dr Coppelius, a geriatric toymaker, has invented a mechanical doll so lifelike that the laddish Franz breaks into his house to get at her. Swanilda, Franz's jealous girlfriend, also breaks in, and watches horrified as Franz is caught by Coppelius, drugged to a stupor, and used in an occult experiment. Swanilda rescues Franz by pretending to be the doll and creating havoc. The pair escape, and then – of course – get married.

Le Corsaire

Young Greek lovely is sold as a slave girl to a lecherous Pasha then rescued by a dashing pirate, who becomes her lover. More hardships follow, including yet another capture and rescue, with pirates disguised as monks. The ballet ends in a spectacular shipwreck with only the happy lovers left alive.

Don Quixote

Ostensibly the story of a nutty old fantasist and his quest for courtly love, the narrative is rapidly overtaken by an irrelevant subplot about a flirtatious girl whose father owns a pub and doesn't approve of her marrying the local hairdresser. One of the most famous scenes involves a band of gypsies, who have nothing to do with either of the above.

La Fille mal gardée

Girl meets boy in a French farmyard where they find a surprising number of uses for a length of pink ribbon. The girl's bad-tempered mother – actually played by a man in drag – naturally wants her to marry the idiot son of a rich local farmer. Young love prevails, but only after the mother has performed her famous clog dance.

Giselle

In a village on the Rhine, a peasant girl falls prey to a local toff who leads her to believe he's an ordinary joe. When Giselle realises she's been had, she drops dead from shock. Chastened, the Count visits her grave only to be hounded by a band of wilies, the ghosts of young girls who've been similarly jilted. Giselle, despite now being a wili, pleads for her man's soul and gets him off the hook.

Manon

Young girl on her way to a convent stops off at an inn, meets a student and runs off with him, unaware that her brother has already sold her favours to a ghastly old man with a foot fetish. Old man tracks her down, offers her a nice fur coat, and she runs off with him. One night, out with the old man, she bumps into the student and plots a second escape, only to be arrested for being a tart and deported to Louisiana where she dies in a swamp.

Mayerling

Crown Prince Rudolf of Austro-Hungary starts off as a syphilitic junkie with a penchant for pistols in the bedroom and meets his match in local bad girl Mary Vetsera. He ends up mad. They both end up dead.

The Nutcracker

Family party on Christmas Eve gets out of hand. Young girl's vision of giant rodents roaming the sitting room and beefcake in uniform are either the result of staying up past bedtime or the dubious attentions of one Dr Drosselmeyer, a family friend.

La Fille mal gardée, Royal Ballet

Romeo and Juliet

Under-age girl meets boy from the wrong side of the tracks. Girl's nanny colludes with crooked Catholic priest to have them tie the knot pronto, then priest procures drugs for girl when going gets rough. Fake suicide pact might have worked if each had kept the other posted.

The Sleeping Beauty

Serious breach of party etiquette brings down wrath of bad fairy on royal household. Despite a palace ban on all things spindle-like, the young princess pricks her finger and falls into a hundred-year's sleep, waking up to her own wedding and a nightmare guest list that includes Puss in Boots and Bluebeard.

Swan Lake

Gloomy young royal seeks solace in field sports and fantasy. Meets an alluring swan who assures him she is really a human magically imprisoned by a giant owl. After swearing undying love, Prince goes off to a party where he gets engaged to a girl who looks a bit like the swan, only she's black instead of white and obviously wicked. He realises his mistake and runs back to the white swan, who ends it all by drowning. Prince follows suit.

La Sylphide

Scotsman in a kilt forms an obsession with a fairy he sees in the woods. A witch called Madge gives him a magic shawl and tells him if he can only slip it round the fairy's shoulders, he can keep her forever. When he does so, the fairy's wings fall off and she dies. Adapted by Matthew Bourne to contemporary Glasgow and called *Highland Fling*.

A Good Read

On the page instead of the stage

For Facts

The Oxford Dictionary of Dance
Debra Craine and Judith Mackrell
Invaluable. The most up-to-the-minute dictionary there is (second edition, 2004).

No Fixed Points
Dance in the Twentieth Century
Nancy Reynolds and Malcolm McCormick
Fascinating, very readable 900-page survey of the major trends and personalities of the century (2003).

Dance Umbrella
The First Twenty-One Years
Bonnie Rowell
Illustrated survey of the UK's major contemporary dance festival (2000).

Fifty Contemporary Choreographers
edited by Martha Bremser
Key figures in today's dance world put in context by 30 writers (1999).

Ballet
A Complete Guide
(originally published in USA as *Ballet 101*)

Robert Greskovic
An informed historical overview with special focus on dance that is available on video (1998).

For Thought

The Creative Habit
Learn it and use it for life
Twyla Tharp
Packed with ideas. DIY manual to creativity (2003).

I Put a Spell on You
Dancing Women from Salome to Madonna
Wendy Buonaventura
An unconventional history of women dancing, including rich portraits of those whose stage antics have earned them lasting fame (2003).

Merce Cunningham
The Modernization of Modern Dance
Roger Copeland
The latest in-depth look at one of the art form's giants (2004).

Insiders' Stories

All His Jazz
A Bob Fosse biography by theatre critic Martin Gottfried (1990).

Balanchine
Bernard Taper's biography of choreographer George Balanchine (1984).

Blood Memories
Martha Graham's musings on her life and career (1991).

Dancing on My Grave
Gelsey Kirkland's harrowing autobiography of a ballerina's life in the fast lane (1987).

Last Night on Earth
Bill T. Jones autobiography (1995).

Mark Morris
Joan Acocella's biography of America's irreverent populist (1993).

STEVEN LAZARIDES

Robert Hylton on top of the Purcell Room

Martha
Agnes De Mille's biography of Martha Graham (1992).

Matthew Bourne and his Adventures in Motion Pictures
Chatty interviews edited by Alastair Macaulay (1999).

Private Domain
Paul Taylor autobiography (1987).

Push Comes to Shove
Twyla Tharp autobiography (1992).

Secret Muses
Julie Kavanagh's biography of Frederick Ashton (1996).

Choreography

The Art of Making Dances
Doris Humphrey
The mother of them all. This practical source book by one of
Martha Graham's leading contemporaries remains one of the
most lucid books on choreographing modern dance (1959).

Modern Dance, Body & Mind
A basic approach for beginners
Sandra Cerny Minton
Learning modern dance technique. Illustrated with many
photographs (1991).

A Widening Field
Journeys in body and imagination
Miranda Tufnell and Chris Crickmay
A handbook for triggering creative juices. The emphasis is on

imagination and receptivity: to our bodies, our surroundings, our materials, and to what we create (2004).

Major British Magazines

Dance Europe (monthly)
Ⓦ www.danceeurope.net

Dance Now (quarterly)
Ⓦ www.dancebooks.co.uk

Dance Theatre Journal (three issues a year)
Ⓦ www.dancetheatrejournal.co.uk

Dancing Times (monthly)
Ⓦ www.dancing-times.co.uk

And a Few Others

Animated (Foundation for Community Dance quarterly)
Ⓦ www.communitydance.org.uk

Pulse (South Asian Dance quarterly)
Ⓔ subscriptions@pulsedance.org

Dance UK News (information and advocacy quarterly)
Ⓦ www.danceuk.org

Juice (information and job opportunities monthly)
Ⓦ www.theplace.org.uk

PRIME SOURCE

Dance Books
The claim to fame for this online supplier is the world's largest selection of books, videos, CDs and DVDs, plus sheet music on all forms of dance. Also rare and out-of-print items.
Catalogue is online or you can request a free copy by phone.
℡ 01420 86138
Ⓦ www.dancebooks.co.uk

Dancing Times
Book and video service. Request catalogue from
Ⓔ books@dancing-times.co.uk.

Where and When to See and Be Seen

UK Dance Festivals

Dance Umbrella

London, September–November

This celebration of international contemporary dance is exciting, revered and a quarter-century young. Umbrella regularly commissions new dances from both UK and international companies.

The festival takes place across London at venues both big and small.

In recent years Dance Umbrella has also produced several national tours featuring select companies.

Ⓦ www.danceumbrella.org.uk

Edinburgh International Festival

Edinburgh, August–September

World-renowned festival of ballet, contemporary dance, theatre, music and opera spread all across the city.

The swank main festival is augmented by the boisterous and busy Edinburgh Fringe, where most of the contemporary dance can be seen in everything from pubs and church halls to tents and out of doors.

Both branches of the Festival feature performances from morning to late-night shows.

Ⓦ www.eif.co.uk

British Dance Edition

A jam-packed showcase for all – or quite a lot, at any rate – that is best on the current British contemporary dance scene. Each year BDE takes place in a different city.

Ⓦ www.anda.org.uk

Nott Dance Festival

Nottingham, May

A friendly and stimulating platform for the latest developments in dance and performance.

Ⓦ www.dance4.co.uk

Hip!

London, autumn

A festival filled with fresh opportunities for black dance artists from the UK and abroad.

Ⓔ hipfest@yahoo.com

WEB INFORMATIONXCHANGE

If you want to know what's on and where to go...

Ⓦ www.anda.org.uk
All of the National Dance Agencies.
Ⓦ www.londondance.com
One-stop shop for dance info in London.
Ⓦ www.WorldWideDanceUK.com
Tours of international companies.

Talk About Dance
Here are the sites to pick up the news and join in debates...

Ⓦ www.ballet.co.uk
Ⓦ www.balletalert.com
Ⓦ www.choreograph.net/forum
Ⓦ www.criticaldance.com
Ⓦ www.dancer.com
Ⓦ www.danceuk.org
Ⓦ www.southasiandance.org.uk
Ⓦ www.worldwidedanceuk.com

CONTRIBUTORS

JENNY GILBERT

is a freelance arts journalist who has worked in television, radio and print. She has been the dance critic for the *Independent on Sunday* since 1994, and is a regular contributor to *Dance Now*.

DONALD HUTERA

is a dance/theatre writer, editor and speaker whose work is featured regularly in *The Times*, *Time Out*, *Dance Now*, *Dance Europe*, *Dance Umbrella News*, *Animated* and numerous other publications. In 2003 he made the dance-based performance *Scary Grant*, thanks to a research commission from the presenters' consortium Guardians of Doubt. *Choreographus Interruptus*, an audience-development collaboration with h2dance, premiered as part of the Nottdance festival in 2004. He and Allen Robertson wrote *The Dance Handbook* in 1988. A new edition will be published next year.

KEITH WATSON

is a freelance arts writer and dance critic for *Metro*. He is a regular contributor to *Dance Now* and *Dance Theatre Journal*.

LYNDSEY WINSHIP

is a freelance journalist and musician. She has contributed to *Dance Now*, *Dance Theatre Journal*, *Criticaldance.com* and *The Independent*, and was joint recipient of the Chris de Marigny Dance Writers Award 2003.